Fire in the Heart

Everyday Life as Spiritual Practice

Roger Housden worked as a freelance journalist and broadcaster, writing features for *The Guardian*. Subsequently, he trained in transpersonal psychology, and ran groups on psychology and spirituality. He also taught the Alexander Technique, and worked as a counsellor for the Bristol Cancer Help Centre. In 1986, he founded the Open Gate – an organisation dedicated to furthering spiritual traditions, psychology, and the arts through conferences, lectures and workshops.

Fire in the Heart

Everyday Life as Spiritual Practice

ROGER HOUSDEN

ELEMENT BOOKS

© Roger Housden 1990

First published in Great Britain in 1990 by
Element Books Limited
Longmead, Shaftesbury, Dorset

Designed by Jenny Liddle
Cover design by Max Fairbrother
Typeset by Footnote Graphics
Printed and bound in Great Britain by
Billings, Hylton Road, Worcester

British Library Cataloguing in Publication Data
Housden, Roger
Fire in the heart : everyday life as spiritual practice.
1. Spiritualism
I. Title   II. Needleman, Jacob
133.9

ISBN 1-85230-133-3

For
Chlöe

Contents

Contents

Preface

The main purpose of this book is to explore everyday life in the Western world as a context for spiritual practice. Part I discusses the fundamental ideas underlying the action and the attitudes explored in Part II. It is intended to be an expression not of intellectual thinking or analysis, but of the living ideas that persist in our hearts. Part II explores how we might act on these ideas in the various conditions of our everyday life. I am keenly aware that any one of the chapter headings in Part II would deserve a book on its own. What is to be found here, then, is of necessity an excursion into matters requiring the persistent work and love of a lifetime.

The book is written for all those in whom some inarticulate question flickers at times in the heart; who, like myself, are unable to espouse the traditional divisions of life into holy and profane, sexual and spiritual, sinner and saint; who prefer to see themselves, rather than as Christians or Buddhists or anything else, as human beings aspiring to live and to die with as much love and understanding as they can bear.

Acknowledgements

I am deeply grateful to the seven people who have given their time and thought to this project by contributing the conversations that are included in the text.
To Ram Dass for being, and for so much help, seen and unseen.
Also to Jacob Needleman for his inspiration and encouragement.
To Robert Bly for singing his longing.
To Chlöe Goodchild for her unceasing love and inspiration.
To Richard Moss, Gabrielle Roth, John Crook, and the many friends who have helped to shape my thinking.
To Michael Mann, of Element Books, who was instrumental in helping me to prune the manuscript into a readable shape.
To Vanessa, who had the patience and enthusiasm to type it all.
To Pierrette and Yann.
To my parents, for everything.

Photo List and Credits

p.12   Photo of Roger Housden *by Chlöe Goodchild*
p.30   Photo of Bede Griffiths *by Carole Evans*
p.40   Photo of Jacob Needleman *by Grayson James*
p.70   Photo of Robert Bly *by Roger Housden*
p.96   Photo of Chlöe Goodchild *by Black and White Studios, Bristol*
p.112   Photo of Kathleen Raine *by J. F. Bonhomme*
p.138   Photo of Ram Dass © *Rameshwar Das*
p.160   Photo of Irina Tweedie *by John Moore*

— I —

The View

Which are the ideas that can stir a human heart?

— 1 —

Everyday Life as Spiritual Practice

I thought the fire was out
I stirred the ashes
And I burnt my fingers.

(*Antonio Machado*)

The spiritual practices of wisdom traditions all over the world are based on the assumption that we are not who we could be. Their overall purpose is to bring a raw set of potentials to their human fullness by applying the heat of certain conditions. Spiritual literature abounds, therefore, with references to 'cooking', to 'ripening', and being 'made good'.

Until quite recently, though, this 'cooking' or 'ripening' would only take place within the confines of a particular spiritual tradition. The tradition was the container within which the heat of the spiritual discipline could do its work. The tradition was, in effect, an oven; and like an oven it worked properly only if the doors were closed. Lips had to be sealed and an authoritarian hierarchy protected the tradition's spiritual technology and wisdom. An absolute and unquestioned world view provided the basis for moral and psychophysical practices; and finally the container, or oven, was sealed off by withdrawal from the affairs of the everyday world.

For people all over Europe, Christianity was for centuries such a container. It offered a complete and definitive view of the universe, and one lived within the constraints and the promises of that view. For those who wanted to enter the fire in earnest, there was the further enclosure of the monastery. Since the Renaissance, however, and especially in the last two hundred years, Christianity has suffered the onslaught of science, humanism, and materialism. Christianity is no longer a sealed container. Its heat has seeped out through a multitude of cracks caused both by the rigidity of its internal structure and by the great winds of change without. Though it certainly continues to be a force for transformation for some, Christianity is being pressed by circumstances to open its doors to the new and the unknown, and to the fact that for most people today the cave appears, at least, to be empty.

The same process of leakage can be seen at different stages in all the world's spiritual traditions. Even Tibetan Buddhism, until recently the most enclosed of all spiritual containers, is now giving away its great initiations in weekend workshops. For good or for ill, the contemporary forces of secularisation and democratisation are forcing open the oven door. The numen, the mystery, is seeping out into the light of day.

Where, then, can we go for the conditions required for the process of transformation? Where else, but also into the light of day? One of the most appropriate vehicles for spiritual practice is no longer so much this or that ancient tradition – even though they may remain an invaluable source of instruction – but the very conditions in which we find ourselves in contemporary everyday life.

The first reason for this is that we live in a wholeheartedly secular age. The ancient custom of withdrawal from worldly affairs in order to pursue a spiritual vocation receives little support from the culture at large. Medieval monasticism could never have thrived as it did if the imagination of the culture which supported it had not been held by a spiritual view of the world that validated the monasteries' existence. The imagination of our time is held by immanent, rather than transcendent values. What matters today is not the hereafter but action for change in the here-and-now arena of both personal and collective affairs. Mother Teresa, after all, captures the public imagination far more than any pope.

We also live now in a world of many relative truths, rather than in the absolute view of any one particular tradition. Spiritual leaders rub shoulders with each other, with artists, psychologists, and scientists, on conference programmes in every Western capital. People can learn Zen meditation one weekend and Sufi dancing the next. With so many answers and methods available, world views that were once considered by whole cultures to be sacred and inviolable are now coming to be seen as relative metaphors. For an increasing number of people, the different metaphors point to eternal truths that are inherent in all traditions. Relativity and universality are developing hand in hand as distinguishing marks of our time.

The very phenomenon of so many spiritual traditions becoming available at once can prise open our minds and help us to look beyond assumed, revealed truth; to look with an eye that is willing to gaze on the unknowable, on the emptiness beyond any static form or belief at all. If there is to be any new form of spirituality, it is possible – even probable – that it will be no more or less than this. We are deeply programmed to expect some ultimate revelation of some kind; some moment or brighter age when all will be clear. Our contemporary task, however, is rather to embrace our unknowing and to live in its consequent wonder and doubt – with all the passion and the insecurity that implies.

The very transience and uncertainty of our culture can, indeed, serve to generate the energy required for contemporary spiritual practice. We live in an unusual age of transition. Without a coherent world view, contemporary Western culture no longer knows where it is going. As well as religion, the other ancient bastions of our security – work, family, and community – are all increasingly subject to the uncertain character of our fast-moving culture. A person may now have several careers in a lifetime, more than one marriage partner, and many changes of address, and even country. Yet we are not satisfied, and we suffer as ever, despite our individual achievements and outer success. All this, if such is our inclination, can help us to see through the promises of this world to one of more enduring values – to another world that is not elsewhere, for there is not, today, anywhere else to turn – but which is within and among the very impermanence and unknowing of our everyday life itself.

The ancient traditions remain great storehouses of knowledge and wisdom, and will continue to sustain us for a long time to come. Today, though, the proving ground for that knowledge is in our everyday secular existence. We start where we are, with who we are, and with the immediate conditions that surround us. What we shall explore here is how the given parameters of our daily existence – relationship, work, nature, the physical body, suffering, beauty – can serve as the grist for our awakening.

The material I have for such an exploration is predominantly the light of my own experience. Our personal experience, and the relative authenticity of our own motivations, are what we are returned to in the absence of an external authority. In isolation, however, personal experience and opinion is no more to be trusted than outward dogma. Authority is emerging today not so much only from within or only from without, but from the interface between the two – from the exchanges we have with each other, and from the mirrors we provide for each other. During the course of this exploration, then, my own experience is mirrored and challenged in conversations with people whose insights and authority I value.

The question of authority is a crucial one and it has a chapter to itself later on. It is part of a larger question still: what are the central ideas that sustain and give meaning to the attitudes and actions we intend to discuss? After all, a way of seeing the world always precedes action of any kind, whether we are conscious of it or not. It is to this question of ideas that we shall turn first – not with an expert or an academic eye, but with the wondering gaze of an amateur (*amatore* – lover) who wants to know more of the truth of his own heart.

— 2 —

Ideas for Our Time

If you were asked to list the ten most urgent needs of the modern world, it is doubtful that philosophy would be one of them. Philosophy, after all, is a world now ordinarily associated with a minor subject of academia pursued by scholars whose concerns bear little if any relation to daily life.

In another, more ancient view, however, philosophy is compared to 'a bite in the heart'.[1] It clings, like an adder, said Plato, 'to any young and gifted mind'.[2] In the Greece of Plato and Socrates, philosophy represented the matrix of living ideas out of which true and effective action could spring. In short, it meant wisdom. We are in dire need of such a guiding matrix today. But what, if philosophy is the love of ideas, is an idea? It is not, if philosophy is to mean anything, our idea of the word as we use it in everyday speech. A wisdom-idea is not a thought, or a concept; nor is it an opinion, or a product of fashion. It is not, therefore, readily available to the rational mind or intellect. An idea manifests as a symbol, or a code, intelligible to a sensitive and awake dimension of the human mind, that portrays an aspect of the truth of the living universe. It works on the human mind by means of resonance, so that the more a person attunes to it, the more deeply it can act on his understanding. There are ideas, then, that have always been; that are shapes of the eternal Truths of the universe in which we live and have our being. Ideas of this stature are to be found echoing through every spiritual tradition on earth.

Why, though, do we need ideas? First, because there is a dimension of our being that loves the Truth, and that depends for its sustenance on the transmission of Truth through living ideas. We are not, remember, speaking of concepts, of concrete pieces of information that we can slot into the jigsaw of our general knowledge. It is not the intellect that is nourished by ideas. It is the creative intelligence, which is the principal point of resonance between ourselves and the rest of creation. An idea is a living thing, and it feeds the living fabric of the intelligent heart.

Then, because a great idea takes us into a world that is larger than our personal preoccupations – because it connects us to eternal principles inherent not only in our own life but in life as a whole – it can impassion us with a thirst for something that transcends words altogether. A great idea can spark a fire in the heart; it can point us towards a life and a path of Truth. To live such a life requires a reorientation of the entire individual, and the re-aligning of the intelligence to resonate with real ideas is a first, though necessary, part of the process. If the intelligence is awakened and turned around, it can serve as a guiding framework within which the further transformation can unfold.

Lastly, the very nature of our time incurs a need for real ideas. We live in a rudderless age of transition, and real ideas are anchors, pole stars that have always been there and are still; if only we might know how to recognise them. That recognition is in large part dependent on the language that is used to convey them. We need a manner of speaking that addresses our present condition and that is echoed in our personal experience.

When we wonder, then, what the relevant guiding ideas might be for our time, it is not that we need to find new truths; rather, we need to cut through the centuries of conceptualisation and self-serving opinion to the living ideas that continue to sustain our lives whether we acknowledge them or not. Faced with even an intimation of the power of a living idea, it is very soon clear how little we actually know at all, despite all the concepts we can muster to our defence. An idea is not something we can grasp, or know about; it is a force that can, as we listen for it, permeate our intelligence and effect a wholly different quality of living.

One great and enduring idea that our time is returning to in its own way is the idea of connectedness, or inter-being:

that we live our lives not as separate individuals but as an interdependent part of the vast stream of living existence. This ancient truth is emerging again through the ecological movement, which is restoring our relationship with the earth; through mass communications and economic interdependence, which are giving us a glimpse of what it might mean to be a global community; through the exchanges between the world's spiritual traditions and the increasing demise of anachronistic dogma; and even through postmodern physics, which has exploded the myth of the solid and separate nucleus.

Another ancient idea that is re-emerging in a number of ways is that the universe is alive; that all matter has its own inherent intelligence and intentionality, and that we therefore live in a world that is sacred – sacred because it is a living expression of an intelligence greater than our own, and normally unrecognised by us.

We shall explore this idea further in the section of Chapter 3 which is subtitled, 'The Living Matter'. Chapter 3 as a whole, however, will address a broader theme that underpins the whole of our inquiry: the eternal idea of the Trinity. In the West, the Trinity has been obscured by the overall degeneration of Christian myth and symbol, and by centuries of literalism and concrete thinking. The Trinity is not, however, a Christian idea; it is a universal one, to be found throughout history, in every corner of the world. On the Capital of ancient Rome stood the Trinity of Jove, Juno and Minerva. Before the foundation of Rome, the Trinity was at the centre of Egyptian, Welsh and Hindu cosmologies. In Buddhism the Trinity, or Trikaya, became the foundation of the Mahayana school. In the 1989 Gifford Lectures at the University of Edinburgh, Raimundo Pannikar traced the Triad through 8,000 years of the history of human consciousness.

This Triad, this animated Three [says P. L. Travers] runs like a bright thread through the true history of the world, from what is highest, to what is lowest, from the most ancient religious teachings down through myth, legend and fairy tale, to the simplest nursery story: – the Trinity which is at the same time One; Brahma, Shiva and Vishnu, eternally creating, destroying and preserving; the Tao with its Yin and Yang, black fish with white eye, white fish with black, united by the encompassing circle; the Three Hidden Splendours of the Kabbalists, roots or principles of the first known laws to govern the universe; Buddha, Dharma and Sangha, constantly wheeling about each other, No-things and yet All-things.

It is impossible not to think of these transcendant Triads in the same breath, as it were, as the three Fates, for as a man relates to one or another of them, so inevitably will his destiny be.[3]

The Trinity, then, is not a remote family of deities in some distant paradise; it is the constellation of energies which make up our whole existence. From moment to moment any one of these forces will be in the fore, directing our attention whether we know it or not. Normally, we are under the influence of the two that create the drama of life, the opposites: light or dark, life or death, high or low, happy or sad, like or dislike, win or lose, man or woman. The two will always oscillate and seem at odds unless a third, less visible, though unifying factor is able to draw the two into one. To become aware of these opposing forces and allow a third one to enter is to see everyday life as a spiritual practice. For we do not have to look any further for the Trinity than where we are. To develop a steady and quiet gaze, however, will be the work of a lifetime.

> You were right, Philosopher [writes P. L. Travers, at the end of her article on the Trinity]. Three is enough – all I need in fact. But can I so live that I can *be* it, that the rival energies dispose themselves in the appropriate order in me? This time it is not you ... but I who ask the question. And as you would surely have predicted, I cannot but tremble before it.[4]

A principal thread that runs through every story of the Trinity is the struggle in man between his longing for the divine, and his love of the earthly; his sense of the eternal, and the awareness of his earthly limits. Much personal as well as national tragedy has arisen from seeing people as only one or the other – spirit or flesh, saint or sinner, sacred or secular. The secret of the Trinity, however, is that while man contains both angel and nature, he finds his humanity, his wholeness, elsewhere: in a third domain which can unite in him the other two. In the next chapter, we shall explore each of these three dimensions in turn. The material I shall use will be that of my personal experience.

Roger Housden

— 3 —

The Trinity Revisited

When God laughs at the soul
And the soul laughs back at God
The Persons of the Trinity are begotten.

(*Meister Eckhart*)

1   This Longing

At the root of much I have done or dreamt of doing there has always been a wish, like some yeast fermenting beneath the skin, for something I cannot quite name. This wish – I would call it a yearning, even – is an inner movement that lifts my attention beyond the daily round to face the eternal and impossible questions that are raised by the simple fact of being alive on earth. It will often persist in stirring and prodding me when I would rather content myself with the familiar preoccupations of everyday life. It will undermine that part of my mind which seeks to find security and contentment in the things of this world – a relationship, a project, a set of ideas, even a religion. It is an innate intuition, felt in the cells of the body, that we are always on the edge of an awesome fullness of life, quite independent of life's contents, that yet, in our habitual mode of being, somehow evades us.

No matter what I have undertaken, or how successful it has been, this longing has ensured that nothing has ever quite been the answer. It has always engendered in me a familiarity with the ancient themes of being awake and asleep, of remembering and forgetting; of having an intimation of some state or being that has always been, that is still, and yet which I am not fully, if at all, in touch with. That which I faintly remember is not of a time past, where it has been rejected by the usual rendering of the myth of the Fall; nor is it somewhere else, in some distant paradise lost far away from the material, everyday world. I know, somehow, that it is in the living present, where I too might be, and am yet not.

All our various desires for this and that, for a better job, a more suitable mate, a more interesting life, all of them stem from this original longing for ... Plato called it The Good: one might also call it God, or Truth, or Understanding. We displace our fundamental wish onto concrete things because the sense world is what seems most real to us, and because what we truly wish for is precisely so fleeting, so intangible, as to make us feel like idiots shouting into the wind.

With the presence of this longing, then, there is a tension and a dichotomy: the tension of sensing unconditioned fullness, essential truth and beauty, just a fingertip away; not quite in reach as I am at present, yet not wholly unavailable either, since I can catch its scent in the memory. This is what J. G. Bennet reminds us of in his book, *The Way To Be Free*, when he suggests that

> Spiritual homesickness is necessary for us. Sometimes it remains in our heart most of the time. There are periods one goes through when one is constantly aware of being bereft of something. When this feeling comes we have to watch over our purity and not misuse it. The feeling is itself authentic and is an indication of being near to something. One doesn't really feel deprived until one is close.[5]

The longing, then, makes us acutely aware of the two directions that co-exist in any one human frame. I remember acutely the moment in my childhood when this fissure, or fault line, first became conscious in my life.

I was out one day walking where I always walked, down across the Seven Acres Field towards Bailey's Wood, crossing the stream on the way. Down by the hazelnut trees, bare then in winter, I stopped as I always stopped to gaze at the green band of hills surrounding me like arms and the lone

The Precious Jewel

All wisdom, according to Daudzadah, is contained in the various levels of interpretation of this ancient traditional tale.

In a remote realm of perfection, there was a just monarch who had a wife and a wonderful son and daughter. They all lived together in happiness.

One day the father called his children before him and said:

'The time has come, as it does for all. You are to go down, an infinite distance, to another land. You shall seek and find and bring back a precious jewel.'

The travellers were conducted in disguise to a strange land, whose inhabitants almost all lived a dark existence. Such was the effect of this place that the two lost touch with each other, wandering as if asleep.

From time to time they saw phantoms, similitudes of their country and of the Jewel, but such was their condition that these things only increased the depth of their reveries, which they now began to take as reality.

When news of his children's plight reached the king, he sent word by a trusted servant, a wise man:

'Remember your mission, awaken from your dream, and remain together.'

With this message they roused themselves, and with the help of their rescuing guide they dared the monstrous perils which surrounded the Jewel, and by its magic aid returned to their realm of light, there to remain in increased happiness for evermore.[6]

---

oak tree that used to fill up with sunlight. I looked, and to my surprise and pain, it all seemed suddenly different that day. I could see the beauty of it all, but for the first time, as an outsider. I was not immersed in it as I usually was. That day, the soft radiance of the landscape seemed unable to penetrate my skin. For the first time, I felt too old for the valley. It was my birthday. I was twelve and I felt as if I were standing on the edge of two worlds. I turned and went back home, not being able to do what I always did, not quite knowing what to do instead.

The sensation of being between two worlds is one that is woven into the fabric of all human experience. It is a pattern whose features were once well recognised and ascribed to various godly forms. Hermes, for example, was worshipped by the Greeks at borders, he being the god of betweens, keeping us to the world and guiding us out of it at the same moment. Eros, however, is the figure who most fully conveys what I am trying to articulate. Eros, the half-man and half-god; Eros the half-god, calling to the half-man. This is our condition, and my life has been a progressive discovery of the two natures, or directions, that co-exist in me, and of the pain that is caused by neglecting either dimension for the sake of the other.

2 The Living Matter

Standing in equal and opposite contrast to the longing that would take me beyond this world, is my love and appreciation of the senses. I know that I am not alone. We all live and breathe the ebbs and flows of the natural world; the rhythm of the seasons and their endless procession of sounds and smells, textures and shades of light. We delight in a good meal; in the vitality of the body; in the embraces of a loved one, and in the feel of the earth under our feet. We are stirred by the sight of a harmonious or graceful shape, and nourished by the light of a fire in the hearth. While the longing wants to move through and beyond all that the eye can see, there exists at the same time the side of our being that already feels completely at home in the world of the senses and instincts.

Pleasure is the perfectly healthy and natural outcome of the interchange between the instincts and the senses with the surrounding natural world. We may imagine that we live in a world given over to the pleasures of the senses and the flesh. However, if our culture appears so pleasure-hungry, it is because it is desperately seeking it in all manner of directions that cannot ultimately provide it.

The more we give credence to the abstractions and fantasies with which the advertising industry fills our minds, the less we are in simple and ordinary contact with our own body and the natural pleasures of the instinctual life. The less we are in contact with our body, the more it seems separate from us, another object to be manipulated for profit and *imagined* pleasure. Far from being a culture of pleasure, we might even wonder whether we might not be one of the more disembodied and anti-sensual cultures of all time.

What our culture is really enslaved to is a continuous outpouring of mental pictures and fantasies that are mere abstractions of the elemental world of the instincts. We barely have to contact the real instinctual world at all: we can satisfy ourselves with our own fantasies, drawing at leisure on the material bombarding us from the mass media. We can be so absorbed in our *image* of the pleasure of chocolate, for example, that we lose all contact with our body and don't even experience whether it actually considers chocolate pleasurable or not. Consumerism is not a result of the body's appetites, it is produced by the artificial stimulation of the mind's propensity for *having* whatever it sees.

The split between mind and body was sealed in the eighteenth century, with the assertion that the human intellect was the origin of all light and intelligence. In one stroke this affirmation deprived all other living forms, including the human body itself, of their own inherent life and light. This is the basis of materialism, which reduces everything to dead matter, of value only in so far as it serves the self-perpetuating and aggrandising drive of the separate human ego, whose principal source of identity is the contents of the rational intellect.

Materialism has levelled the multiple network of living beings to the horizontal plane of utilitarian values. It has stripped the world of its gods, its life, and its beauty.

Salisbury and Hart, in an article entitled, 'The Evolution and Future of American Agriculture', use language that encapsulates the materialist attitude. They see it as a major sign of progress that 'the dairy cow has changed from the family companion animal she became after domestication and through all of man's subsequent history, into an appropriate manufacturing unit of the 20th century for the efficient transformation of unprocessed feed into feed for man'.[7] It is through attitudes and language like this that we are causing the devastation of our own habitat. Whereas for millennia, humanity has venerated the Earth as nurturing Mother and lived and worked in intimate relationship with its moods and seasons, the currently emerging figure of Earth is that of the poisonous and devouring Matriarch: the one whose air we dare hardly breathe for fear of the pollutants we might inhale; whose seas are dying and casting bloated fish on the shores; whose forests are giving way to burning deserts that cannot sustain any life. All this, because we have forgotten that matter is alive; that it breathes life into us and that it is the living foundation of our highest aspirations.

The natural world is screaming out for a new response: that with both our aesthetic and our moral senses we celebrate, respect and care for living matter and that we recognise our interdependence with all living forms. The pulse and rhythm of the Earth regulates our heartbeat just as it determines the season for the falling of leaves and the sprouting of seeds. The world of nature begins with our own body. We dare no longer envisage it with eighteenth-century eyes, as if it were the troublesome appendage of our all-seeing mind. Neither does it serve to see it with the tired eyes of our mainstream Christian heritage; as the cumbersome baggage of a divine spirit whose home is elsewhere, and whose call it deflects us from with all its temptations. On the contrary, we need to wonder whether the body itself might be a source of the fullness we are seeking: a source not only of our instinctual fulfilment, but also of that Presence which may pervade, and yet transcend, the instincts themselves.

If we view the body in this way it is as sacred as any holy

place. It is not merely a container for something greater, other, that may enter it; it is itself the source of the pervading, immanent presence of life. It is not a vehicle for the essence that we truly are: it itself is who we are, though not only who we are.

It is for this reason that sexual intimacy can be one of the most sacred and mysterious acts known to humanity. Through the body, it is two beings that can merge, and the more the partners act and respond from the spontaneity of being, the more they can be taken up into the mysteriousness and wonder of Being itself. The act of bodily love is a way for us to extend beyond the confines of our separate sense of self and to touch the deepest layers of our existence. The degree to which this is possible, however, depends in large part on whether we have healed the mind–body split of materialism, which has reduced sexuality to a commodity and a sensationalism stripped of heart and intelligence.

To envision instinctual and sensual life from an aesthetic and moral standpoint is not, however, to deny the essential characteristic of matter that ascetics and philosophers have struggled with since time immemorial: its inherent capacity for limitation and restriction. To refute this would not only be a futile attempt to spiritualise or sentimentalise matter away; it would deny its fundamental value and purpose. The body, after all, is subject to degeneration, suffering, and inevitable death. Humanity aches and groans, shivers and splutters, almost as a matter of course, as well as suffering all manner of desperate conditions that bring it staggering to ignominious death. Before the vastness of life, our hearts and minds, too, are cramped into a tiny corner of experience and knowledge. Finally, the greatest ideals towards which we may aspire will always be limited by the given conditions of a particular situation.

The question is not how to override this principle of limitation, to idealise it or romanticise it out of existence, or to reject it as some lower state we are soon to leave. The limitation of actual physical conditions acts in direct counterbalance to the seemingly limitless potential and aspiration of the human spirit. The question is how these different dimensions in us might come into relationship with each other in such a way as to form a full and integrated human being – one who is equally at home in either world and who is consequently subservient to neither. For an answer, we must look to another qualitative level than either of the ones we have already explored.

3   The Presence

The borderlands are twilight zones that generate a heightened attention; shady places where identity is never certain and where the true and the false, the legal and the illegal, intermingle and are easily confused. The borders hold a certain excitement, an anxiety as well, for here the familiar and habitual edge up to the strange and the new and reveal each other in a fresh and unusual light. It is the same with the interior borders that run between our various states and levels of being. A tension is generated that is greater than the intensity of either pole alone when we become sensitised to the simultaneous existence of apparently contradictory forces.

The seam running along the edge between the experience of our limitations and our sense of the possible is one that collects more psychic energy than most. This energy is usually dispersed in any of a number of ways: we might be drawn into inertia by the weight of the obstacles, or compelled into action by the drive to do something, anything, to improve our lot; or we might fritter away the energy of the conflict by day-dreaming.

Somewhere in the midst of these more usual movements there lies another way: the willingness to gaze without thinking, or analysing, or doing anything at all, into the experience itself; into the very essence of our humanness. The activity of beholding what is before us is a direct matter of the heart, of the clear region in our being that is willing and able to contemplate things – ourselves – just as they are, without adding or taking anything away. It is an activity of gathered, though gentle attention; not the attention of a pencil light, that separates figure from ground, but rather the diffuse light of a candle or taper that allows everything to rest in its setting. In the light of this attention everything changes. What was a struggle seems to transform into a relationship. It is not that we miraculously become as we would like to be; it is that a shift occurs in our adopted posture towards ourselves and the situation we are in.

In the presence of this attention, a person's whole idea and sense of themselves loosens; they are less fixed and permanent altogether; less conscious of being a solid subject wrestling with the dilemmas of either the inner or the outer worlds. Instead of having a point of view, they become part of the view itself. It is not that one becomes self-effacing, or that one disappears; one simply resumes a proportionate place in the pattern of things. The quality of feeling that emerges is one of spaciousness. There is room, plenty of room, for the arrival and departure and changing of shape of the phenomena that emerge on the horizon of the mind or of daily life. This is so, because within the presence of this kind of attention, there is no story-line, no hidden agenda with which to attempt to orchestrate life.

This does not mean that a person does not care what happens. It means that, bearing their burden more lightly, they care in a different way. It does not mean that they do not act. Their activity becomes part of the larger activity of an overall situation and its related qualities and forces. In the presence of this attentive dimension of heart, a person will still act, but the initiative seems to stem less from a subjective me-ness than from a movement deriving from the overall need of the pattern of relationship.

This kind of action is compassionate; it is less concerned with gaining a specific end than with playing a part that asks to be played. It is an action which is not the result of thought, of considered choice, so much as one that, as it were, does itself.

This sane, awake quality of presence that can stand between and gather together our contradictions is a doorway into our wholeness – into what is truly individual in us. It constitutes a third force in man and woman; a force we might dare to call soul: not the natural soul of existence that imbues all living forms, but the distinctly human soul that is a creation of intentionality, of conscious, if subtle effort. The word soul itself rings uneasily in contemporary ears. The literalising tendency of memory and intellect has handed us down a notion which conjures the image of a concrete entity living inside the body and that will survive its death. Perhaps it was in part to counteract this literalism that Buddha taught that there was no such thing as 'soul' at all.

Ultimately, perhaps all vestige of selfhood is extinguished completely. We in the West, however, are steeped in the value of the individual. It is the shadow of that value, not its truth, that we see rampant as the cult of individualism. At the deeper levels of Western spirituality, the Person has always represented the intermediate level between the frag-mentation of ordinary consciousness and its illusory sense of a unified self on the one hand, and the ultimate fusion with God, or the Void, on the other. This final union was recognised by, among others, Eckhart, who nevertheless spoke of the realisation of the Person, as the major step on the way.

There are some transpersonal psychologists, such as Ken Wilber[8], who seem to point to the realisation of this Person-hood when they suggest that a self must be actualised, developed, before there can be any self to give away, or see through. They suggest that the healthy development of the ego is an integral intermediate stage on the way to full self-liberation. Yet the ego, however healthy, remains in the confines of the temporal, subjective world, and transforma-tion is not a developmental but a disjunctive movement – a shift between worlds rather than a linear progression from one stage to the next. It is the soul – that which is truly individual in a person – which constitutes the reality of the Person, not the healthy ego. The soul lives on the edge of the worlds; it is a dynamic, an intelligent constellation of silence and energy. It is individual precisely in the sense that it is a presence that can remain unswayed before the desires and aversions of the subjective self.

Yet this individuality is not something separate and independent from the rest of existence. Since it lives in a realm beyond the opposites, it is not a personal subject that relates to exterior objects. It exists by virtue of both subject and object, self and others. With its origin in the interaction of both, the individuality of the Person, as we use the word here, is peculiarly both individual and common property at the same time. We can sense this sometimes when we see into another person's eyes and become aware of someone truly there; and at the same time realising that suddenly there is also someone who is really looking. In that moment there is a unity which does not incur a loss of self but a gathering of different selves into something greater, or more, than either. When two or three or more are gathered in the name of its presence, everyone becomes more individual, more close to who they are in truth; and yet they are more united to each other, more as one, than ever they are in their familiar and separate subjectivity.

It is the birth of the Person, then, that can occur through the bringing together of earth and sky, the desire for the transcendant, the Beloved, the fullness of things, with the daily experience of life in and as the body and the senses. It is through the eyes of this Person that the secular is made sacred and the many become one.

— 4 —

On Whose Authority?
The Interior Heart and Sacred Tradition

Who is it that can recognise this Person in themselves or in another? And on whose authority can this recognition be confirmed? The Western spiritual heritage has always mistrusted, even feared, the authority of subjective experience. In the monastic communities mystical experience was not encouraged or favoured; daily work and the communal liturgy were the rules of the day, and the ecstatic songs and visions of a John of the Cross or a Teresa of Avila were the exceptions and not the rule. As a result, Christianity finds itself sadly lacking in methods and practices of contemplation, and without the formidable and sophisticated psychological maps of Eastern traditions, whose foundations rest on empirical observation and practice. Our own spiritual heritage is thus ill-equipped to serve us in an age which places great emphasis and authority on the value of subjective experience.

Personal experience is increasingly becoming the litmus test for views and attitudes that have for millennia been considered inviolable. Sacred cows and dogma are falling as never before. Clearly, with the demise of traditional forms of external authority, confirmation is sought from within and in such a polymorphous culture as ours, all kinds of views are tenable and possible. We live in a time when it is feasible to subscribe to any one of the spiritual traditions of the globe, to several of them at once, or even to one of our own making.

In valuing so highly the authority of personal choice and experience, then, what are we actually giving value *to*?

In this age of the personal, three different strands of subjective authority need to be distinguished. The first is the authority we have bestowed on the value of experience itself. We value experience so highly we will do anything to 'gain' it: job experience, life experience, sexual experience, mystical experience, peak experience. We have become addicts of intensity, climbing the highest mountains, running the fastest miles, making the quickest million, seeing the finest gurus, doing the most meditation. In the temporal world of quantity, experience is indeed invaluable. However, we attempt the impossible when we try to storm the qualitative realm of the unconditional with the quantitative values of the temporal. More than a few of us, and most of us at one time or another, go about gathering 'powerful experiences' like so many collectables we can check off on some spiritual curriculum vitae.

We might well wonder which position we are covertly aiming for. In the measure that we equate the intensity of the experience with who we imagine ourselves to be, in that degree we are prone to inflation and to a lamentably unrealistic view of our actual condition. It is this that has always stimulated the wariness of tradition, both East and West. Intense experience can indeed be a way of reaching our personal limits and falling through to a broader expanse of realisation. At one time or another, it is almost certainly necessary. But the essence of spiritual experience is not so much something one gathers, as it is a process of peeling away the layers of the person one thought one was, of sorting one's own wheat from the chaff. Then, without the kernel of understanding, the husk of one kind of experience may be of no more use than the husk of any other.

The second kind of personal authority is that of personal choice, the great prize of modern democracy. We are free to choose which channel to watch, which country to live in, and now, in the full-blown polymorphism of our time, we can decide which spiritual tradition to follow from the worldwide selection available on our doorstep. It is also our prerogative to select a variety, a bit here and a bit there, or indeed to make up our own concoction on the spot. The choice is ours.

Whose? Mine. Whose? In truth, the decision often goes to whichever preference or opinion is uppermost of the several in the mind that are clamouring for attention.

There remains a third form of inner authority in which the event or situation in hand seems rather to choose me than me it. Though one may appear to be making a choice, one is in fact confirming, or naming, a process which is already wanting to occur. The naming of the process does itself, however, take courage. It implies a commitment; making a stand for something or someone, not even because one necessarily wants to, but because it is what needs to be done. One's action is thus the conscious outcome of a relationship of circumstances. Seeings what one sees, one can only act in the way one does. And yet, paradoxically, this kind of action is a true expression of freedom. For this seeing is not of an ordinary kind. Action arising from it bears a stamp of something enduring, more substantial than the vicissitudes of personal preference or opinion. It is like this with a real marriage, or with the commitment to a particular spiritual group or form of practice. In Buddhism, it is insight that makes visible what was previously hidden by our own obscurities. In Christian terms, we return to the ancient theme of conscience, a word all but emptied of its original substance today and reduced to being associated with guilt and cloaked authority figures behind confessional screens.

Conscience essentially refers to the eye in the heart of hearts, the interior heart in which we know what is true and how the truth needs to be acted on. This heart is the silent region which is interior to, or anterior to, the heart of the emotions and passion. It is almost as if it were a subtle organ of perception which joined us to the pulse of things in general, and specifically to the heart of the matter in question. The knowledge of the interior heart is not a personal affair alone: it is a current that runs through the filaments connecting all the various components of the situation at hand, including oneself. For this current of knowledge to flow unobstructed, the log jams created by personal feelings and preferences and unrecognised drives, need to be freed.

There is much talk nowadays of following and listening to one's heart. In my case, it is not difficult to confuse this with following my personal inclination. Unless we can distinguish the logs from the river, we are never likely to go with the current, which, along with its silence and simplicity, is always an uncompromising and impartial master.

The voice of interior conscience has always had the exterior sounding board of a sacred tradition to echo it. Though spiritual tradition has often served to repress rather than acknowledge individual insight and vision, it has also acted as an objective body of knowledge and authority against which the individual might assess the authenticity of his or her own inner voice. It has also provided the framework within which this inner authority might arise in the first place; for such authority is not simply there as a given of existence, as something the personality can turn to whenever the trouble it has caused itself is too great for it to manage; it has to be cultivated through intention, through persistent and patient practice. It is in this area, in the provision of such a context for the development of inner authority, that the Western tradition has gone to seed, and that the Eastern traditions have rushed in to fill the breach.

Buddhism, especially, makes available teachings and methodologies that provide an objective mirror for personal insight, as well as the means to cultivate it. Just like any other spiritual tradition in our culture today, however, it does not and cannot have, the voice of absolute authority. The era of absolute truth is over. The aberrations and idiosyncrasies of all traditions become plain when they rub shoulders as intimately as they do today, and even more so, when many of their foremost representatives, especially among the Buddhists, have proven, in the context of our permissive culture, to be as prone to human frailty as anyone else.

We live, then, in an age of responsibility: a responsibility for ourselves but also for each other. The demise of absolute authority is both an opportunity and a terrible danger. The danger is that we shall give authority to our preferences and secret ambitions rather than to the word of the heart. The opportunity lies in finding the strength to affirm the voice of our own conscience. It also lies in the giving of authority to the spiritual community. One of the principal gifts of various traditions today is the context they provide for people of like mind to put their will in the same direction. Others of like mind, and the community as a whole, can reflect to us the validity of our personal understanding.

In our time, spiritual communities are regrouping themselves in many forms within everyday society itself. One may even be part of a community which has no name, whose members are spread all over the globe, and yet who recognise each other instantly on meeting. Whichever community one is drawn to, even if its numbers are no more than two or three, one of its primary functions must be to re-mind one of one's deepest aspirations; to reflect the clear mirror of the interior heart. This is the purpose of the spiritual friend, or friends, without whom the journey is a difficult and treacherous business.

It is for this reason that there are other voices in this book besides my own. I would count them all in their different ways as friends who have helped me to keep my own questions alive. Some of them I have met on only a couple of occasions; but they have all, either in words or in their manner of being, illuminated some truth about myself or about our collective situation that I had not seen before. My conversations with two of these people make up the rest of Part I of this book. These two very different men have been instrumental in helping me articulate some of the more obscure thoughts and feelings that have long inhabited the borders of my conscious world. They are Father Bede Griffiths and Jacob Needleman.

Father Bede Griffiths

— 5 —

Father Bede Griffiths

Bede Griffiths, in his eighties, is tall, spare, and radiant; an English monk who lives in a straw hut in southern India and who wears the saffron robe of the Hindu renunciate. He has lived there for decades, and is happy to know that he will die there too. Having lectured and travelled all over the world, he has not moved out of his ashram, Shantivanam, for several years now, and has determined not to do so again. He has come home. Home to his beloved and impossible India; the land that has enabled him to sound the depths of his own Christian tradition and to perceive the universal essence enshrouded in its metaphors.

This is the reason I went to see him. In writing this book I could see the unmistakable imprint and language of my own Western culture. It surprised me, then, I who had never felt myself to be Christian, to see the pictures painted by my own words – the Trinity, the Person, and so on. This, in someone who thought they had received more from Buddhist practices and techniques than ever they had gleaned from their native inheritance. I wanted to know the significance of these metaphors from the perspective of the tradition to which they belonged.

It was to Bede that I turned because I knew from his books and from mutual friends that he had pursued his faith as a living question. Not content with dogma or doctrine, he had allowed himself to be shaped by the spirituality and the people of India as much as he, in his turn, had made an impact on them. The church at Shantivanam is indistinguishable from a Hindu temple, open on all sides, with carvings of the four evangelists looking like Indian gods. Shantivanam is an ashram that serves the local community as a centre for

Hindu Christianity, and the community of *sannyasins* (renunciates) as a place of work and prayer. It is under the authority of the local bishop, and is affiliated to the Camaldoli Order, whose principal monastery is in Rome. Father Bede left the English arm of the Order, Prinknash Abbey in Gloucestershire, thirty years or so ago to make his own interfaith experiment at Shantivanam. The monks go to Rome to join the Order and the larger Christian community, but they then return and take the Hindu sannyasin vow of renunciation of all communal and brotherly ties for the sake of their solitary flight to God. Thus the Christian emphasis on community and the Hindu's concern for individual salvation are brought together in one place.

Father Bede sees people all day, one after the other, in his little hut. It struck me how freely he gives of his time and energy to all who ask for it: not just to those who live alongside him in his ashram, but also to the many who come from all over the world to stay a week or two, or even a few days, in his oasis of tranquillity in the tumult of India. He is available, though, not out of some idea that he should be of service, but, so evidently, out of a surfeit of life and unpremeditated generosity.

His hut is filled with a bed, a chair, a small table and some books. I sat on the bed. Who was I sitting with? Who was he sitting with? Neither of us knew much more than what was before our eyes. I began speaking about the finite and linear worldview of Christianity, and how incompatible it seemed with the emerging idea in the West of relativity. How could the Christian metaphors and their language of an absolute revelation possibly meet the emerging needs and climate of our time? He leaned forward in his chair.

'When I first came to India, you know, I was incredibly Christian. Gradually I have become more open.' He spoke with a smile on the edge of his lips, as if an early memory of himself had just passed through his mind. 'I always remember a brilliant theologian from Sri Lanka saying that the church had four attitudes to other religions. First, all other religions were false, Christianity alone was true. Then, by the eighteenth century, when they began to know a little more, they proclaimed that all other religions were natural and Christianity was supernatural. Then, in the nineteenth century, it was said that other religions have elements of the supernatural but Christianity was the fulfilment of all other religions – which I held for a long time. Then, he said, the fourth is the complementarity of religions – that each religion is a unique expression of the one infinite truth, reality. That is what I hold today. And that, I think, is the challenge to Christianity.'

'The challenge, then,' I ventured, 'is to embrace the paradox of apparently contradictory truths – the Buddhist not-self, for example, and the Christian idea of the Person.'

'Yes.' He looked up at me, and our eyes met. 'But paradox has always been inherent in Christianity. Eckhart is a great witness of it, as Cyprian Smith explains very well in his book, *The Way of Love and Paradox*.[9] And then Nicholas of Cusa, in his wonderful *Vision of God*, speaks at great length on the conjunction of the opposites in God. Paradox is difficult for the conceptual mind, but it is familiar ground to the intuitive. Eckhart speaks of the two aspects you mentioned as the God and the Godhead. Sometimes one prays and uses the language of duality, and from there one can fall into a silence. Then, as Eckhart puts it, beyond the Persons of the Trinity is the Unity, the Godhead, as distinct to the personal God whose Presence one may long for and feel at times. The Godhead is the void, the empty desert. In Mahayana Buddhism, however, the void is absolutely full. In that One, every particle, every electron, subsists. In Hinduism, too, there is *bhakti*, love in relationship, and *jnana*, love of wisdom, without an object. I find both accessible, and I do not find the contradictions a difficulty.'

The lightness, the transparency of this man, was beginning to dawn on me. I asked him what prayer meant for him.

'In the ordinary Christian sense,' he replied, 'prayer is *bhakti*, devotional song and praise to God. There, one is still on the level of images. *Jnana* is to go beyond images, beyond the psyche to the divine spirit itself. This would be contemplation, which for me is true prayer, an awareness of the

Presence. This is the kind of prayer that we tend towards in this ashram. All other kinds of prayer are means to come to this experience of what is beyond all forms. I differ from St Benedict in this. The Benedictines focus on the liturgy, several times a day. Now I know from my own experience that this can be a very deep practice, but still one is always using words and concepts. In India, any liturgy is both an expression and a nourishment of a deeper form of contemplation and leads towards that deeper form. Silence is always the eventual aim.'

'Does that silence have, or need to have a name?' I asked.

'God is the Nameless One, but every religion symbolises that. Christ is such a symbol, the sacrament of the Holy Word. If you are a Christian, I see no difficulty in giving the name of Christ to the intimation of that nameless Presence, realising that the name is a symbol for that Infinite Transcendence and which, in a way, we express when we say that Christ has a human nature but is also divine. It's very deceptive this language. Human nature is something we know, but there is not properly a divine nature at all – it is the absolute infinite unknown.'

'So you are saying that the human nature of Jesus is one with the Infinite Beyond?'

'So many Christians absolutise Jesus. I really don't equate Jesus with God,' he continued. 'If you look through the New Testament you will see how they carefully avoid speaking of Him as God, but of a person through whom God works. People are beginning to re-awaken to the inner mystery of life now, but how are we to name it? We can use the language of any spiritual tradition as long as we recognise that religious language is symbolic. This is just what we have not done for a long time. Protestants have absolutised and therefore made an idol of the Bible, and the Catholics have done the same thing with the Church. The Church has put all these mysteries into definite formulae, three persons in one, and so on, and the formulae have become mere conceptualisations of a mystery which cannot be reduced to words.'

'If we were to shake the dust out of the formulae, what would we see?' I asked.

'We would see the beautiful idea that the Trinity, for example, is Perikoresis, dancing love. The Father, the origin, gives himself to the Father and this 'self giving' is the Holy Spirit. When two people love one another, they go out to each other, lose themselves, finding a unity beyond themselves and within themselves. That is personal relationship, which is the model for all relationships – a unity which goes beyond the duality. The Trinity is the unity beyond the duality.'

'Yes,' I said, 'because the whole is greater than the sum of its parts. The two are apparent, while the third is within the two, while not of the two.'

'How difficult that is to grasp,' he replied. 'It simply has to be experienced.'

I was awake now, far more attentive than when I had first entered the room. I asked if Christianity was the only tradition to point to relationship in this way. He replied that it was in both Hinduism and Buddhism as well; that in Buddhism the Void is not static, but a dynamic out of which the whole Creation issues forth. At the very moment of issuing forth, however, it returns. Within this apparent duality is the unity of the Void.

In Hinduism, there were many forms of Vedanta, but the most interesting to him was Kashmir Shaivism. There Shiva was pure consciousness, Shakti pure energy. Then there was the vibration, the consciousness, that went between the two. So there again was the two and a third which went beyond the two. So each religion pointed to the reconciliation of the opposites.

'These opposites are the stuff of our life, you know,' Father Bede continued. 'There is the mind, consciousness, and there is Shakti, energy, which needs to flow. We block it however; some block it at the physical level, some at the head. If it can flow, however, Shiva, consciousness, and Shakti, energy can unite and you have male and the female in one.'

'Allowing it to flow means not getting caught by, attached to, the phenomena and experiences of a particular level?'

'And not rejecting it,' he replied. 'The tendency in

Hinduism, Shankara especially, is denial, though the other systems of Vedanta correct that. We all tend to one extreme or another. Shankara's world emphasised pure knowledge, wisdom; our culture is obsessed with sexuality. How to go between the two, while including both, is the question.'

We paused for a moment. The bright Indian light made us shift our positions. I began again on a different tack. I wanted Father Bede to explain what he meant by the word 'person' when he spoke of the Persons of the Trinity. He replied slowly, as if thinking over his words while speaking them.

'Karl Rahner maintained that the modern idea of the person is not valid for the Trinity at all. For us a person is a being with its own intelligence and subjectivity. There are not three persons in the Trinity, if you use the word in that sense. There is rather a process – a process of outflowing of the Father to the Son and the Son back to the Father. In the original understanding of the word, the Person is relationship. This is the essence of the Trinity – the persons of the Trinity are a set of living relationships. It's like Fritjof Capra's description of the universe – a complicated web of interdependent relationships.'

'So you are upholding an image of process as distinct to one of a concrete object?'

'Yes, relationship is the dance, the movement itself,' said Father Bede. 'All that was originally in the Christian doctrine of the Trinity. Subsistent relationship, as Aquinas called it, is the essence of the Person, and is embodied in the Trinity. So often the ancients had the most profound insights, which became lost as the language they used lost its connection to the movement of the times.

'The conceptualisation takes over,' he went on. 'I always remember the story of the man who was being instructed in the Catholic faith. He was asked how many persons there were in the Trinity, and he said, "There's the Father, there's the Son, and . . . I am afraid I can't remember the name of the other gentleman."'

Father Bede paused for a moment, and then continued.

'Bergson was someone who saw this clearly, how the conceptual mind objectifies, makes things separate from each other, whereas Reality is flow. This the Buddhists understand, and this is why we Christians have such need of dialogue. We need to recognise the limitations of the biblical revelation, as well as the Christian development of it.'

I asked Bede what he felt Christianity had to contribute to present-day dialogue with other traditions.

'Above all,' he said, 'the historical dimension. If you leave out history, as Buddhism and Hinduism tend to do – after all the Buddha was one of an innumerable stream of buddhas – you lose the person, the historic being. In Hinduism, there is the One to which you all return, but you do not realise your personal being. There is not, then, relationship as such. The ultimate is pure Unity. In Buddhism, it is a unity which flows but still there is no personal communion. The Christian Trinity is a unity experience of dynamic relationship in ultimate Reality. This, I think, is Christianity's most distinctive contribution to this current meeting of world faiths. Our founder once said that our whole aim here at Shantivanam is Advaita in the Trinity – how to relate non-duality with the Trinity.'

Both of us sat back. We had come to a certain completion. Neither of us, however, got up to go. The cawing of the crows in the palm trees reached my ears for the first time since I had entered the hut.

'Is there anything you feel to be left undone in your life?' I asked, almost casually.

Father Bede replied immediately. 'I am making the discovery,' he said, 'that I have not fully realised what Nicholas of Cusa calls the resolution of the opposites. How to relate to the little details of life, for example, is something I have not understood.'

'What kind of details?'

'Like the problems of the body, whether to take a medicine or not, what food to eat, all the stuff of the daily round. I have for much of my life been concerned with getting beyond all these things, and now I am seeing the need to get down to them. Perhaps, in the end, I will get right down to them!'

'And take yourself a wife. . .?'

'Well, in a way everyone becomes your wife, you unite

Purusha with Prakriti, male and female, within yourself. It is the wife in oneself I am speaking of.'

'We seem to be speaking of the redemption of the body,' I said. 'Whereas the more normal Christian view has been to see the body as an unfortunate encumberment.'

Father Bede sighed. 'Yes, what a tragedy that is. Tantra has saved Hinduism in this respect. My whole orientation now, you know, is to get to the base of the spine, to get to the roots of life, and not to soar off into the sky.'

Jacob Needleman

— 6 —

Jacob Needleman

I first met Jerry Needleman in Senanque Abbey, one of those twelfth-century Cistercian monasteries that still survive in Provence. Senanque is a model of plain beauty; pared back to the simple stone, nothing unnecessary, spread out in a field of lavender between two great ridges of white rock and thistle. We were there for a conference on meditation in everyday life. Jerry was at the conference to give a paper; except he didn't. He was the only one to speak without notes, pondering his words, and feeling his way into what we were all asking. I don't remember what he said, but I do remember what he did. He was alone in that conference in not giving any answer. Instead, he used his ideas to evoke in us the yearning and the questions it raises. People were stirred; but then so was he – these questions were for him, it was obvious, the stuff of his life.

That evening we continued to talk. He is a stocky man in his fifties, with a broad, mid-European face. He could come from Vienna, or Budapest, perhaps. His forefathers probably did; he, though, is from a Jewish background in Philadelphia, and has lived in California for thirty years. He told me more of the story behind the book, *Lost Christianity*, which had inspired me to come to the conference in Senanque. I had never read a book quite like it. Here was someone who was asking questions of our spiritual heritage that it has rarely had to face. How can I possibly love my neighbour when my more normal experience is a lack of love? What are the steps required to move from an absence of love to love itself? Has there ever been the knowledge in the Western spiritual tradition that can provide these steps?

Several months later I attended one of Needleman's classes

at San Francisco State University. He has been Professor of
Philosophy there for twenty years or more. It was an extraordinary experience to witness 'philosophy' being taught
that way. He was bringing alive in the minds of twenty-year-
olds questions that will nag at some of them for the rest of
their lives. Afterwards, in his house near the university, I
asked him why, after all these years, he was still so evidently
fired by the value and importance of ideas. He answered in a
way that brought to mind our time in Senanque; his words
were measured and slow; yet they came with a vigour, an
intensity, that can only be present when a person is wholly
engaged in what they are saying.

'Ideas,' he answered, 'are spoken to the mind, but they
touch the heart. This is why ideas are especially important
today: people live in the mind, mostly, and they need to hear
something that is spoken to the mind, even though it pen-
etrates deeper than the mind. I don't think the language of
faith, or myth, can carry truth in a way people can hear
today. There are at least two elements in us that are instru-
ments of deeper knowing. There are others, but there is
certainly a compassionate mind and a knowing heart. It is to
these that real philosophy must speak.'

'How would you distinguish the activities of these two?' I
asked.

He was silent for a moment. 'When one stands before the
greatness of Nature,' he said at length, 'or looks into another
face sometimes, or at death, there can arise an impulse, a
need to understand. Not so much that I need to do anything
about it, but that I need to understand. That, I believe, is the
mind of the heart. Sometimes the heart in the mind, to point
a difference, can be very passionate, very excited. But it is not
necessarily touched by great truths in the way the mind in
the heart is. It is moved, rather, by something which excites a
passionate interest – that wants to solve a problem, for
example; to make a scientific discovery, to play the piano.
The mind can be very emotional about things like this. So I
want to distinguish that from what we might call yearning.
The yearning for what? Not to do anything in particular, or
even to be anything, but to understand. This is the nature of

the heart-mind. This is something I would describe as a sacred impulse. Philosophy can touch that, although most philosophy today does not.'

'In which way can philosophy touch the heart-mind?' I asked.

'It can evoke it,' Needleman replied. 'You look at the stars, and you experience a sense of wonder. Ideas can do that. They can evoke a sense of wonder, and quiet the ordinary mind. When the mind is really quiet, what we might call genuine feeling can be heard. Sometimes that feeling might be the wish to understand. Philosophy can give you a glimpse of this; it can help you recall something in yourself that you've forgotten, in the absorption with everyday life. It can make you stop and be present for a moment and sense more closely who you are. This is why Plato called philosophy remembering. It helps you to remember, and then you forget again, you forget who you are. Ordinary life draws on certain functions in you, calls you by a certain name, gives you a social identity, all of which is essential. But it obscures the call to wonder who you are, beneath all that. Philosophy is one of the means by which human beings are called. It is the art of remembering.' He paused for a moment, and then continued. 'There are some, however, who will never be reached by philosophy; they may be moved by something else, by art, music, religious language. Philosophy is only one of the means of communication from the higher down to us. There is then the question of how the great ideas of philosophy can become a lived experience, and for that you need a path, a guide, and the understanding of how to engage in inner work. Philosophy does not, and does not pretend, to do that.'

We were now reaching the territory that I had really come to explore with Needleman. How could great ideas become a lived experience, and, in particular, the idea of the Trinity?

Needleman sat back in his chair, absorbed and reflective. When he spoke, his words were barely audible. 'If Jesus Christ had to live and to die on the cross in order to fully incarnate the three forces of God, we can be sure that the work of experiencing the deepest meaning of the Trinity is going to be not only a task to which we are all called but a very difficult one. We maybe need to ask how we understand this idea of the Trinity. Why is there, just on the level of ideas, why did God put Satan in the Garden? It was God who put the serpent there – he didn't just crawl in from outer space. And who created Satan? This is part of the idea of three – something moving in one direction and something opposing it. Good and Evil were both created by God. It must be, then, something that is intrinsic to all of reality, the Threeness of things.' He looked up at me. 'Can you find it in your own experience?' he asked.

I replied that I could see two apparently contradictory forces in my life – the need to understand, which always wanted to look beyond or through the form of a thing; and on the other hand, the appreciation, the instinctual contentment, of being in the sensory world. Usually my experience was of being in one world or the other; occasionally, though, through a certain kind of intentionality, those two worlds come together in a third condition that was able to embrace them both.

'It's not always easy,' he said, 'to identify these two worlds. Sometimes the wish to understand is not so pure. The very thought that this is a finer movement, towards God, for example, is already the beginning of the other world.' His voice was firm now, and bore an unusual authority. 'The mind comes in so quickly and identifies something as of one world or the other. But is it to be trusted? The ordinary mind, after all, will serve all manner of masters. So above all else, we need to develop the power of impartial observation in order to know when we really do go from one world to the other; the witness, the capacity for just looking. The mind itself is part of the resistance. It doesn't always serve the Good. That is why we need this observing faculty. All this, by the way, is certainly not philosophy. It is already the way. There are moments when we experience this witnessing accidentally – in great crisis, in sudden shock, in great joy, or for no reason at all. These moments show us what is possible, though they are just the tip of an iceberg. That taste of presence, though, is the touchstone. We can't go by intellectual objective criteria, but by the personal taste of when we are present. All this is to say that this great idea of the Trinity cannot really live for us unless we have the taste of what it means to see, through having cultivated the faculty of attention. Unless we have that we are in danger of turning a great idea into another sleeping pill, which is what happens to all great ideas. I would even say that a spiritual path is one that understand the inner and outer conditions which allow this taste, this seeing, to appear more often and more deeply in all conditions of life.'

How often, I wondered, in the silence that followed Jacob Needleman's words, had I known that taste of which he was speaking? To know that state of seeing, one must have the wish for it. The wish itself is so easily lost and confused with all our other various motivations. 'How can one possibly touch something authentic in oneself', I asked, 'when almost anything we do has an element of inauthenticity in it?'

He laughed. 'Absolutely,' he replied, starting forward in his chair. 'It's impossible. So we start with that awareness – I don't know, it's impossible, I'm confused. Being aware of that one becomes quieter, and as I become quieter, I see that I needn't be afraid of confusion. It's the truth, and I begin to see I need to stay in front of my confusion, without my impatience. If I move around too much I lose even the question, so if I really value that wish in me for understanding, I must be quieter. I need a quieter body, I have to have less distractions, I have to try and stay in front of that, and I see that I can't.

Then that begins to be my question. Something in me wishes because in that moment my mind remembers. I know that moment when life had more meaning; when I was present there. So my mind has an important function to play there, one which is the real work of the intellect: to remember what was experienced in that moment of presence – what was felt in the body, and so forth, which at this moment is not being experienced. But the memory starts to gnaw at me: don't you remember what that was like? This can help me to come back again to see that I don't know where I am or who I am. So I begin to see that I keep losing that. All the ideas of God, religion, and higher states, I see are really secondary for now, because until I am present to myself, aware of the truth of myself, those other things are going to be just fantasies. So my question comes down to where I really am. I see I lose myself and the question in all the activities of my life. So we know now what we need to try and do. We need to come back again and again to this awareness of my confusion, of the impossibility. Yet in that awareness,' Needleman continued, 'in that listening to the confusion, something begins to open up, and I don't know how. The work is not about God, or infinite love, it's about being alive, open to what I am now. It's impossible, so I stop trying, but I don't stop wishing. How to wish without doing, how to let the wish act without passing through the part of myself that always wants to do something? That is a kind of intentional suffering, because everything in me is wanting to do things, and all that part suddenly has to become secondary. It will resist that because it is not used to being secondary. So we need to allow that part to exist without swallowing us. It needs to learn that it has nothing to be afraid of by allowing itself to be watched. It needs to be found its proper role within the wholeness of ourselves. Its function is very important, but it is not the master, it is the servant.'

'In saying that,' I replied, 'you are setting up an opposition . . .'

'Absolutely . . . that is the way the Trinity enters.'

'So', I continued, 'there is the automatic part of ourselves, there is the wish . . .'

'And there is the third principle, which accepts and which is in touch with both; which is not hostile to the automatism, and which is not in love with the wish. If you're in love with the wish, then the automatism just comes in the back door. Even knowing about this idea of the three principles is of the greatest help, because it helps me to work. At a certain point I have got to let go of the idea, because the idea itself can get in the way. But without that idea I would never have known how to work.'

Before we ended our time together I wanted to turn the conversation to one other theme, the question of presence. Here was another word that we both used quite frequently, and I asked him for his understanding of it.

'I was in a near miss situation in my car,' he replied. 'As the other car was coming towards me I felt there is nothing I can do, it looks like I'm going to die. In that moment, "I" appeared; and "I" didn't want to die, but I was not afraid, the presence of this "I" allowed me to function with extraordinary effect. Time changed, almost disappeared; there seemed to be a great deal of time in which to act, and it simply was it, it was not afraid.

'To take another example, I was fourteen-years-old, walking down the street, and suddenly I stopped completely in my tracks: I heard my name being called, and I suddenly realised, "I exist!"'

'These are accidental moments,' I interjected. 'What of moments intentionally evoked?'

'They are the same,' Needleman answered. 'But there are laws by which we can make room in ourselves for such moments to occur. And I would say that this is always trying to take place in us. The Higher, the Presence, whatever you want to call it, is always reaching down, wanting to enter into us. It is we who set up the obstacles to it. Nervous tension, for example, is an obstacle, a tense body. So we need to understand what real relaxation is. For when this Presence appears, it does so in the body, not just the mind. We need, then, to cultivate a certain quality of sensation in our body, that allows the body over a period of time, to be permeable. There's a way of living, a way of working, that can help this.

'If you meet a man of great presence,' he continued, 'and you just happen to brush against them physically, you can't help but notice how wonderfully flexible their body is. And you just know that something is inhabiting their body which is more than the usual tensions and cravings.'

'So there,' I said, 'with this presence being felt in the body, is the coming together of two disparate worlds.'

'Let's make no mistake, though,' Jerry Needleman said quickly. 'That coming together is on the whole preceded by a certain kind of intentional suffering – that of being willing to see how far apart these worlds are in our common experience. This is no easy task. Peace, the peace that passeth all understanding, is not some insipid tranquillity; it is that which brings together two completely opposing and warring forces. These forces really do oppose each other. The body is not the spirit's world. They can come together, but only through seeing how far apart they are. When you see and suffer that you are not what you wish to be, and you don't try to change it or cover it up, that is conscious, conscious suffering. This is the fire that really brings the two together. This is alchemy. We must always beware of the easy synthesis,' he continued. 'I wouldn't wish this fire on my worst enemy, but it is the only way, because you see yourself as you are. When a Christian speaks of remorse, or tears, this is what they mean. That what they know to be the Good is resisted by something in them. There's nothing else to do but simply suffer that and pray. It has all been twisted in the teaching of sinfulness, but this is what it means at heart. Gurdjieff speaks of the wolf and the lamb, and how our aim should be to care for them both in ourselves. The wolf will eat the lamb unless the man is there to keep them in their respective domains. At the back of Notre Dame Cathedral is the sculpture of a leery devil putting his arms around an angel, and the angel is graciously embracing the devil. Behind them both is this figure, much taller, of a warrior watching them. It is under his gaze that the two come together.' Needleman paused for an instant. 'Then, and only then,' he said finally, 'can we begin to have some intimation of what love might mean.'

— II —

The Means

— 7 —

The Practice of the Presence

Those who want Me, I will give him all sorts of troubles
in this world. If he will not mind these troubles, then I
will give him all sorts of pleasures in this world. If he
ignores these pleasures, then only will he have Me.

(*Krishna*)[10]

Jacob Needleman left me in no doubt as to the depth and the
manner of seeing required in order for the Trinity to become
a lived experience. What, though, is the arena for that
seeing? It is the conditions of our daily life. We shall begin by
enquiring into what is already there before us, the humdrum
events of any day. By enquiry, I mean the practice of an open
gaze that is willing to look at what is before it, without being
deflected by the inevitable judgement, fear, preference or
boredom.

In the case of our internal condition, it will not take long to
see that what is normally there is the posture and assumption that we know what we are doing and who we are as we
go about our daily life. If we stop and look a little deeper,
however, then what begins to appear is our manifest ignorance: I do not know what any one single thing really is, least
of all myself. At the same time, there is a yearning to know.
This is a genuine starting point from which I can begin to pay
attention to my everyday life in a new way.

What connects me and my inner condition to the external
world are my senses. In giving attention to the way we use a
particular sense faculty, we begin to discover a depth and a
source of life in the simplest and most common acts of daily
living. We can begin to pass through the outer layers of our
senses, which remain on the surface of things and of people,
to an ever-deepening sensitivity that joins us intimately to
the moment we are in, and to the people and place we are in
relationship with.

The eating of a meal is a familiar activity that engages all of our senses at once. It may not be a coincidence that it has always been a sacred symbol and sacrament in religious traditions all over the world. How often it is, though – far more often than not – that a meal passes by unnoticed. Even our favourite food is often consumed without any real awareness of what is occurring. And yet with just a slight, though not easy, shift in our awareness, we can eat a chocolate mousse, for example, in a way that can give us a wholly different appreciation of it. Conscious of raising the spoon to our lips, and sliding it into the mouth; the dark, almost musty smell of chocolate in our nostrils; our own anticipation of the pleasure to be digested; the smooth, creamy texture on the tongue and against the palate, reducing it almost to a liquid as it slips down the throat. What happens when we pay attention in this way is that we somehow go beyond our sensation of pleasure; beyond like and dislike altogether, to a state of presence in which the specific sensation of personal gratification transforms into a more general state of greater aliveness.

It can be the same with food we do not like. Conscious of raising the fork to a mouth that only half wants to open; the dark green of cabbage, perhaps; its odour hitting the nostrils, the teeth chewing the leaf, cutting it up, breaking it down; the taste and the juice of the vegetable filling the palate . . . Normally, we are so identified with our like or dislike of a given food that our opinion of it allows little or no room for any awareness of either ourselves or the food. By paying attention to what actually happens in our various senses as we take a spoonful of food into our mouth, we separate ourselves from our reaction of like or dislike *without* rejecting it. This separation creates a space in us which can allow a third condition to enter.

Our senses, then, can be gateways on to the fullness and Presence of Life. How rarely, though, do we really see; we listen, but we barely hear; we touch, but we know not what we touch. If it is to be otherwise, it is essential that we engage with the world from the standpoint of open and wonder-ing inquiry. We shall explore the sense of sight in this way in the chapter on Beauty. Here we shall take the examples of touch and hearing. I take hold of someone's hand, for example; someone I may hardly even know. What is it that I am touching? I do not know. What is its texture, the temperature, the wetness or dryness? In this contact there will probably be an automatic response in me of either attraction or aversion. This is wholly natural; but if I follow either response, I will not be able to move any deeper. My enquiry will have ceased. We want to allow room for something that stands beyond and between our like and our dislike. What is it then that is just below the skin that I am touching? In gripping, I feel it one way; in holding the hand lightly, I have another kind of connection. The other's weight and substance brings me into contact with my own, and shows me the degree to which I myself am actually in touch with the part of my body that is touching them. Then in touching, we are touched. We may sense the tremor of a sadness or a joy in the hand we are holding and feel the same emotion passing through ourselves. Still, if we let our emotion pass on we shall discover there is farther to go. Conscious touching – be it with a person, a flower, a piece of wood or a stone – is an invitation to an unusual kind of intimacy. It is not the intimacy of shared emotion, nor that which moves us into a pleasurable, even erotic exchange with another. It is the intimacy of a shared presence, beyond desire, that is sufficient and complete in itself. Such intimacy as this transcends gender. It dissolves the barriers of separate selfhood, and yet gives a person some intimation of the fullness they can be. There, in that intimacy, we are in touch with the ground – of ourselves, of the other, and of life.

To touch and to be touched in this way, however, requires time. We cannot be in a rush and expect to pass through the layers of another's skin as we would pass a knife through butter. This kind of intimacy requires respect and humility, and the clarity that comes with an absence of sentimentality. When we first touch a rose in this way, or the carcass of a cat by the side of the road, we are before a mystery that may or may not reveal itself. If we allow a romanticism to capture us on the one hand, or our distaste on the other, then we obscure what is before us and allow no room for the situation to speak to us more deeply. The fact is, we obscure the content of our lives in this way most of the time. If we even begin to see that this is what we do, we may open the door to another possibility.

It is the same with listening. Usually we hear two-dimensionally; sounds ricochet off our skin, returned to their source unrecognised. Or they activate the membranes of our judging mind and trigger reactions that convey an impression quite other than the original sound itself. It is a prerequisite, before attempting another kind of listening, that we know this to be the case. Normally, we simply do not listen, especially to the people and the things we want to hear. How often have we really listened to the voice of a loved one, to birdsong, or to the wind? We are more often aware of the sounds we recoil from – an ambulance siren, loud music in a restaurant, chattering voices. It is not a question of self-recrimination or blame; it is our condition. There is also that in us, though, which longs for the unconditioned; and we need to hold these two natures in us alongside each other in order to listen differently.

In a certain way, this really does seem more possible with a sound that we react against. After all, it seems more feasible to stand aside from something we do not like, and the holding apart of our aversion and our listening is fundamental to a deeper learning. A sound I instinctively react against is that of thumping music in a restaurant. I feel it prevents me from being attentive to who I am with and to what I am eating. It disturbs my stomach and makes it difficult to digest my food and I just cannot understand why it has to be played. The more I try and blot it out the more irritated I become.

If something in me can just have the presence of mind to notice – no easy task – that I am being totally controlled by the music, then something else becomes possible. Instead of resisting it I can allow the sound to be there; I can make contact with my body and my breath, and my feet on the floor. I can relax the tensions in my body; I can hear the rhythmic beat; I can hear the sounds in the restaurant as a whole. I can simply remind myself what I am doing every now and then by repeating the word, listening, listening. What can happen is that my discomfort may begin to change and a more spacious way of being can emerge. The music is still there, and it still jars; but my relationship to the situation has changed. Nevertheless, I only take up the challenge when I have to: I still look for restaurants without loud music.

I still follow as ever the sounds that attract me. I derive great pleasure from the wind and the rain and the crackle of wood in a fire. I love to hear a sonorous voice, and music of a kind that, like Gregorian chant, elevates my spirit, or that returns me to my instinctual roots, like the repetitive work song of some ethnic tradition. I am an example of what Jerry Needleman points to in our discussion: I love to fall in love with the longing itself; and with the unconditioned celestial realms. I am strongly attracted, then, to anything that will get me there, be it the wind or uplifting music. Sometimes, though, I know that the land of truth lies farther along the way. Sometimes, something in me is able to glimpse how my energy is totally wrapped up in the object or sound that delights me – or rather in the pleasure I am deriving from it. At that moment, I can begin to hear the wind in a different way. The images and associations it had conjured up in my mind begin to fall into the background, though not always out of sight. My whole body becomes an ear, and what is heard, distantly, I can only describe as essence of wind; raw wind, shorn of all the adornments of my emotional and mental descriptions. All there is – everything there is – is the play of sound, and the vivid awareness of it.

How easy it can all sound in print. Can this degree of attention really be expected in the busy and preoccupied life of the contemporary world? Rarely. We simply have to want to make time for it. We will make time according to the intensity of our wish for a life we suspect can exist, but that we do not experience in the way we habitually live. The gap between our actual experience and our sense of the possible causes a pain, and this pain, bitter-sweet, generates the engine of our desire for another quality of living.

It is a quality, though, that we may suspect we shall never

fully realise. Though we may arrive at a state of attention in daily life that is already a big step away from our habitual consciousness, we can sense that the step we are making is just one on an infinite journey. The Presence we may catch a hint of, while potentially present to us in any moment, is infinitely beyond our reach and ken. There will always be a deeper Mystery to life than we can know. Why, then, begin in the first place? Because our sense of being alive depends on it; and because, in the end, we can't help it. This impulse, which is sacred, lives in us whether we wish it or not. We follow it – or the memory of it, which is more often the case – for the simple love of it all. What else, after all, can we do, in a world where every other desire will eventually fall by the wayside, seen for what it is, a finite husk?

— 8 —

The Body

God guard me from those thoughts men think
In the mind alone;
He that sings a lasting song
Thinks in a marrow bone.[11]

Yeats knew that no wisdom endures which does not pervade the cells of our body. It is not difficult to speak or write wise words; it is another matter to live them. Whatever we may say, our body stands as living proof of who and how we are. Our deep attitudes and the quality of our feelings shape the energy that we express in our body.

The mirror for me of my own living proof was the Alexander Technique. The lessons were sobering indeed. I discovered I was stiff-necked; that my lower back was pushed in and my chest stuffed out; that my pelvis, not my feet, thrust me into the world, and that I had the posture of receiving life squarely on the chin. What all this suggested was that, despite the precious philosophy I held of 'letting go', of 'going with whatever arises', I was in fact someone who was clearly dominated by the struggling mode: by the tendency to be preoccupied with the particular end in view and to be striving towards it, with no great regard for the means I was using to accomplish the end. In this, I was a typical specimen of our goal-oriented culture in general.

The natural rhythm of my body had been usurped by the ambitions and desires of my self-concerned personality, which was drawing the instinctual energies of the body wilfully upwards to aspire to the particular end in view. My centre of gravity was lifted into the upper chest, inflating it with a varying degree of self-importance, anxiety, and re-activity. The protruding chest and the arched back that supports it are together attempting to sustain and present a picture of myself to the world as one who can 'take it'; who can win through, who is 'somebody' of substance. The self-importance grows out of my believing my own story. The anxiety is there because it is all rather hard work. There is considerable tension involved in holding oneself and one's world up in this way and, furthermore, a residual instinct tells me that this whole posture towards life is dangerous: it is encouraging me to lose touch with base, with the ground, and with anything authentic in myself.

What is motivating all this tension at root is the fear of its opposite: collapse. The hypertension of the typical Westerner is sporadically punctuated with periods of exhaustion and illness. The posture folds in on itself, head lolling, back slumped, legs splayed. There is the sensation of lack-lustre, lifelessness, no will or wish to go anywhere or do anything. There are many for whom this is a normal experience of living. Rather than the centre of gravity being displaced upwards, it has in this case dropped through the floor. If the tension of the first posture can be seen as a Herculean attempt to assume responsibility for everyone and every-thing, then extreme slackness, its opposite, can be seen as an image of the bumbling anti-hero, a Woody Allen; the one who feels barely capable of 'shouldering' anything; who finds all and everything just rather too much.

For me, it was not only the Alexander Technique but also meditation that opened the door to a condition that is relatively free of these two extremes. Alexander began by showing me where I was, and then went on to indicate an altogether other way of living and moving. I had practised meditation for some years before training as a teacher of the Alexander Technique, and I had long been familiar with the 'idea' of 'not doing' – of allowing the transformation of events and of mind phenomena to occur spontaneously through an intentional attitude of 'letting them be'. Yet it was only through Alexander that I really began to understand what 'not doing' meant. It was a real delight when I realised for the first time what it felt like to let an action do itself – to let the walking walk me. The physical sensation of myself was – is – radically different in this condition to the way I experience myself in either of the polarities of tension or collapse.

Rather than feeling like a taut string on the one hand or a slack one on the other, there is in this case a 'tone' in my body and life; a movement and a flow which engenders a sense of being properly tuned. I am relaxed, but alive, streaming, even; certainly more receptive and permeable to ideas and sensitivities of feeling that a tenser or a slacker body would have been opaque to. My head has dropped forward a little and resumed its natural balance on the top of the spine, because my neck is no longer so concerned with holding my head 'above water'. My chest has returned to a sense of proportion, so my back is less arched; my coccyx has relaxed, so my buttocks no longer protrude as much as they did. I am less self-conscious, too, and my centre of gravity is located not in the upper, but in the lower chest and the navel. I have dropped down into myself; I have become embodied. The sensation is one of lightness and presence; the feeling, one of relief.

Though the Technique restricts itself to the efficient functioning of the physical organism, both the bodily awareness and the attitude it engenders have deepened and intensified my understanding and practice of meditation. However, while the Alexander Technique runs the danger of imposing some imagined picture of 'right posture', meditation and the practice of just sitting have come to affect me physically from the inside out. It is evident in everyday life that different moods and attitudes are carried in their own particular physical postures. In the same way, I have increasingly noticed when 'sitting' that my body subtly shifts according to the degree of openness and availability in which I find myself. The more tense or slack I am, the less there is any meditation at all. The more openness and depth of feeling there is, the more I experience spontaneously what Alexander does through intent. The chin drops, the spine lengthens, the shoulders drop, the chest widens. It amazed me when this first happened quite dramatically and suddenly, as if my body has been seized by the state I was entering. It was like an inner realisation and confirmation of what I knew through an external technique. More normally, the movements that occur are far too subtle to be registered by an observer, and are reflections of the many gradations of falling into silence. The inner condition and the physical releasing serve to catalyse each other. As the shoulder cracks open a tiny degree further, so the attention heightens and deepens, which results in the head coming a fraction more into balance on the top of the spine, and so on.

The temptation is to try and set it all up to begin with. Many a meditation teacher is to be seen adjusting the posture of his pupils. The difficulty is that there is no right posture for openness, attention and availability. Clearly there are guidelines that need to be followed: it is not easy to be open when slumped in a chair or with one's legs folded around each other. Yet what needs to be done is not simply of a mechanical nature. One has to start where one is, in a recognition of one's tension and slackness, of one's dispersion or over-intensity, and be open to being moved, literally, from within.

It may then be discovered for oneself how various postures, gestures and localisations of energy and attention, which are taught as systems of yoga and even as contemporary therapeutic techniques, have their origin in spontaneous physical manifestations of inner states of being. This is to approach the body and movement from a quite different direction than many of the current body work techniques. It is a direction indicated by Archbishop Bloom in dialogue with Jacob Needleman in the latter's book, *Lost Christianity*.

I [Needleman] asked Metropolitan Anthony again about the work with the body, about the methods, the exercises I knew were in the Christian tradition – somewhere, in some time. Where did they come from? Where have they gone? I waited for him to continue. He said something about the Athonite Christians having this work with the body, and then paused once again.

Finally, he raised his eyes towards me. 'You have been to our service. If you stand in the service with your hands down to the side, with your head slightly down – not too much – your weight evenly balanced ... if one does this, one begins to see changes taking place in the body. The breathing changes, certain muscles relax, others become firm, not tense. All this comes from the religious impulse . . .'

Again a pause.

He continued, speaking softly and deliberately. 'The exercises you ask about originated in this way: from the Fathers observing what happened to them when they were in a state of prayer.'[12]

The experience of the body falling into place when imbued with the 'religious impulse' can have an echo in the way we go about our daily life. Through the experience of being shaped in meditation, a physical memory is developed of a bodily state of being that can engender a state of presence and availability in everyday life. I say physical memory, because it is held not in the brain but throughout the body. The shoulder 'knows' to open; the breathing 'knows' to descend. By intentionally falling into the physical shape of openness and presence, it is possible to express these qualities with a degree of authenticity. If the self-conscious mind attempts to assume a stance or attitude of openness, or act according to some preconceived ideal, it is difficult for the adopted posture to be any more than posturing. If the mind drops down into the body, however, and lets the body lead with its more concrete form of remembering, then we are likely to be more true. The body, after all, is always present, always here where we are. The more we enter into it, the more we fall present too. As the body becomes softer and more receptive, so it is more disposed to being moulded by the finer energies of life into their more accurate reflection.

Being moulded in this way does, however, require an invitation. The bodily remembrance I have just described is the expression of an intention, and constitutes a formidable practice when committed to on a regular basis. Other physical practices are more specific and more obviously, the vehicle of a certain kind of effort. The commitment to bring sensation to a particular part of the body at regular intervals during the day, is one such practice: bringing one's attention to the chest, for example, and becoming aware of all the sensation there. That such a deceptively simple task can not only bring one back to where one is, into the present moment, but can also, with a sufficiently living intention, generate an awe and wonder at the larger Presence of life, is itself a testimony to the body's mysterious power.

There are, however, less intentional ways that the body enters into spiritual practice, far more wild and ecstatic than this. Every now and then, for no reason, I have found myself breaking into a dance or a run that will continue for what seems like an eternity, even though it may be for no more than five minutes. Sometimes the dance will be chaotic, sometimes slow and serene. Either way, I will not know what I am doing. It is the dance that dances me, not the other way around. Occasionally, moved by some suitable music, I will find myself turning on my axis with my arms out wide and my head to one side. This is one of the most ecstatic, abandoned movements I know, and yet it requires at the same time the presence and subtle discipline of attention. As the physical body opens to the world, the inner attention remains gathered in the silent region of the heart. If I lean too far either way, I end up in a giddy heap on the floor. The turning is nothing less than a bodily song, a love song, uttered with the whole body in unison.

This may almost be a description of the act of making love; and in a way it is. Through the dance one is making love with life. It is the body that has the remarkable power to gather us back into One: to fuse into one direction the disparate energies of thinking, feeling and willing. Only in and through the body and feelings may the whole person be moved; a task we normally and mistakenly imagine to be that of the wilful and self-conscious mind, with all the consequent tensions and imbalances of contemporary life.

— 9 —

Nature

In wildness is the preservation of the world.

(*Henry David Thoreau*)

How can our relationship with the natural world be a vehicle for awakening? We often speak of nature today as if it were the preserve of either the conservationist or the romantic. We refer to the environment, and to the 'eco-system', as if Nature were an extension of our living room, to be regulated, monitored and serviced at regular intervals in the same way as our central-heating system. Either that, or Nature is mentioned in soft tones verging on the sentimental; she is our Mother from whom we have turned away and whom we need to learn to love again. Both these perspectives point to truths that are urgent for our time; in the same instance, they both run the danger of depriving the natural world of its own power and vigour by reducing it to purely human terms.

Nature still bears an awesome majesty, terrible and mighty, with impetuous and unpredictable moods and whims that have always, until recently, struck fear into the hearts of men. Insulated by glass and concrete, by cities and cars and streets and planes, our ancient fear of Nature has gone underground, into the subterranean alleys of the unconscious. With it, we have buried our respect for Nature too, and our knowledge of the meaning of awe. For our ancestors, the voice or the vision of God would leap out of a stormcloud, or would appear in the desert; it would strike into the heart with a bolt of lightning, or it would speak on a mountaintop, far above the tame and peopled valleys. The feelings of awe and dread are holy feelings because they bring us into the presence of the numinous; of the almighty and the unknowable. It is in Nature that these feelings might still be found.

I live on a small and domesticated island with manicured hedges and footpaths across gentle hills that carve the sky into manageable pieces. No dangerous or wild animals survive, and it is utterly safe at night. I was first afraid of the elemental world somewhere on a mountain overhanging the sea in northern Greece. The path, such as it was, wound along a steep slope of loose scree that plunged some hundreds of feet into a rocky sea. Every now and then the path petered out in the descending forest of twisted and stunted pines. The loose stones and the beauty I was surrounded with made my progress slow, and night began to fall long before I saw any sign of the monastery I was heading for.

I was on Athos, a finger of land that juts ten miles into the sea, which has no roads and no signposts, and no human habitation except the orthodox monasteries that have been scattered along it for well over a thousand years. When the sun went down I was picking my way among trees with no means of finding my bearings. I heard the call of an animal. Could it be a boar? Surely there weren't wolves in this region still? I had never met a wild animal in my life. The nearest we come in England to any such thing is a fox or a badger. The unfamiliar and sudden sound brought every pore of my skin alive; not just to the presence of possible danger but to the rippling power in everything around me: in the stones, baked in the sun for thousands of years; in the southern light, which even at dusk caught the edges of things and cut them into a chiselled relief; in the trees, spiralling alchemies of all the elements; and in the wind, which was starting to gather in sweeping gestures, any one of which could toss me into the sea in a single swirl. I hovered between fear, excitement, awe and dread. More than at any time I could remember I felt alive; alive as an integral member of a vast network and circuit of Life and Death; of an eternal rising and falling of an infinite number of forms.

The raw and uncompromising force of Nature serves to chasten and strip away the polish and accretions of culture – the protective layers with which we insulate ourselves from the truth of our own condition. The desert has always been the principal symbol of purgation; and not, I have found, without reason. The first time I went to the desert, in this case the Sahara, it was to live out a dream. My plane touched down at Tamanrasset airstrip in darkness and I spent the couple of hours before dawn in the little passenger building talking to a mountain of a man with a handlebar moustache who was on his way to Chad to hunt rhinoceros. As the rocks began to glimmer in the first light of dawn, I clambered into the jeep that was to take us to town. We bumped down the track and within a few moments the Sahara was unveiled to my staring eyes: a vast rolling moonscape of red rock and dust streaked with the purple and yellow of the emerging day. The sun that was rising over the furthest crags was larger than any sun I had ever seen. As it lifted itself higher into the gaping sky the rocks burned redder and threw their stark relief against the canvas of blue.

After a couple of days I found an Arab guide who was ready to take me out into the desert and return for me three days later. This was my dream – to know what it was like to be alone out there far from all trace of humanity. After a day's ride we came to some rocks that would provide some shelter from the relentless sun. Saïd left me a goatskin of water and rode off with our camels back along the ancient river bed. As I watched him go I became aware that I had never before put myself so straightforwardly and unthinkingly in another person's hands.

Within a day the drama and excitement of acting out a long-cherished daydream had evaporated. No longer was I playing the lead role in some movie. There I was, alone in the midst of this desolate landscape, awoken each morning at the first glimmer of light by swarming hordes of buzzing flies, churning out the same ordinary thoughts as I did back in Kilburn. Their mediocrity, my own mundanity, stood out starkly in the unswerving stare of the desert sun. I found myself beginning to laugh. I was no great ascetic, meditator, visionary, or ecstatic; there was nobody very special hiding beneath my daily round waiting to be revealed; no reserved destiny or Damascus experience waiting to proclaim itself on the desert stage. No, beneath the habitual tick-tock of my hopes and fears, past and future, there was nothing to speak of at all; simply a sense of clear and empty space.

On my last day alone I walked far out from my rock into the

empty expanse. After some while I stopped and looked back over the way I had come. I seemed to have walked no distance at all. My footprints had already been filled by the shifting sand, and there was no evidence of the effort I had made to come this far. Suddenly, there in the implacable light, I was stripped of all self-preoccupation and artifice and bared to an awareness of the deep insignificance of the personal melodrama that I imagined to be my existence. In that moment the emptiness without shone as a mirror for the emptiness within; the living desert became a picture of my own innate condition. Standing there, a speck on a vast canvas, I felt true, authentic, and unashamedly small, without even a story to tell.

The desert and the mountain are wild places, where the throb of our instinctual nature is more easily registered than in the places we normally frequent. Without their assistance we might all but forget that we ourselves are half wild. Perhaps we are more than half wild, for we are dependent upon reflexes, instincts and appetites that we do not cause or intend and that we cannot, or had better not, stop. Then, among the daily chatter of the psyche, we might hear in some quiet or unsuspecting moment the distant roar of a wild man or woman deep down inside us; one with flying and flaming hair whose urge is to leap out and break the chains of our habitual life of conformity. With the progressive closure of acceptable means for this voice to join in our civilised life, it increasingly emerges as a brute which blindly erupts in meaningless violence and destruction. All this is to say nothing of the wildness of the spirit; the mad yearning for who can say what; the self-abandonment of a Zorba in praise and celebration of Life itself.

We have tamed the wildness in our culture almost to the point of extinction. Our inner and our outer wilds are squeezed behind walls and fences into ever-diminishing spaces. Yet we know from agriculture that our domestic needs depend on a balanced co-operation with wilderness. It is worth quoting Wendell Berry here in full.

A forest or a crop, no matter how intentionally husbanded by human foresters or farmers, will be found to be healthy precisely to the extent that it is wild – able to collaborate with earth, air, light and water in the way common to plants before humans walked on the earth. We know from experience that we can increase our domestic demands upon plants so far that we force them into kinds of failure that wild plants do not experience. Breeders of domestic animals, likewise, know that when a breeding programme is too much governed by human intention ... uselessness is the result. Size or productivity, for instance, will be gained at the cost of health, vigour, or reproductive ability. In other words, so-called domestic animals must remain half wild, or more than half, because they are creatures of nature.[13]

We humans are creatures of nature, too, and we forego our wildness at our peril. I suspect that as we domesticate our more primal nature to the degree that it becomes an entirely unconscious activity, we cut ourselves off from the bare truths of our soul and spirit as well. In some unrational way our instincts are sluice-gates through which the authentic feelings for Life – awe, dread, wonder, marvel, joy, sadness – can pour. If we let these gates fall into disuse then we are likely to confuse fantasy and delusion with spiritual power and insight.

None of this is to deny that domesticity is also of value to the wilderness, and that we are domestic creatures by nature also. The task is always to generate a third quality, not given by nature, out of the wildness and domesticity with which She has formed us. A tree is the stronger and healthier for a seasonal pruning, and to take a creature who is biologically human and to make them fully human is a task of a lifetime, possibly even more. A human being must be made, and this long effort of human making is a cultural process doubtless necessary because of our power. Out of the interaction of the two forces can arise a quality which can crown them both, and which is, in its own way, a special kind of love. The fox in St Exupery's *The Little Prince*, told the Prince that he could only become his friend by 'taming' him. A Persian friend of mine once spent a winter alone manning an isolated army outpost in the hills of Northern Persia. One day, as he was crossing the frozen river on the way back to his hut, he came face to face with a wolf. He was unarmed ... helpless. They gazed at each other, motionless, for a long while, my friend uttering a silent prayer all the while to the wolf, that he might spare him. After an age, the wolf turned and went by another way. That night my friend heard a scratching at the door of his hut. It was the wolf, who, in the harsh winter, had probably not eaten for days. The man gathered some food, and let it fall out of the window.

I have only spoken so far of the extraordinary side of Nature; of far-off lands; of light and jagged edges; of mountain and desert; of stony, burning ground, of wildness and intensity. I speak of these things out of a certain preference, I admit, though not, I hope, in order to dramatise either Nature or myself in colours that are more vivid than life, but because I believe that these are the aspects of ourselves, in Northern Europe, at least, that we have become most unfamiliar with; that we have projected on to the gaudy posters of the tourist agency, which sells our wildness back to us in the packaged safety of a ski slope and a five-star hotel, and of camel rides in some emasculated desert corner. There are a multitude of other faces, faces that also live in us, which Nature reveals far closer to home. There are, right under our noses, the mud and the rain. My first reaction is to shrink from both. But what am I shrinking from? Mud oozes, and squelches, and is alive with crawling things. It sticks to our shoes, and makes us less presentable. It is messy, uncomfortable, and inconvenient if we have not prepared for it. Our preparedness, however, is our polish, our civilised face. I find at times that the presence of mud can slip under that skin and reveal a secret delight in oozing disorder; that mud returns one to one's own earth; to one's own humour, humus, humility. It is the same with rain, especially the kind which pours in sheets. It wipes the make-up from our face, disturbs the hair and drenches our finest clothes. When I am willing to see it this way, which is certainly not always, I am able to appreciate the enthusiasm of Kabir, a poet-saint of sixteenth-century India. He said (via

Robert Bly's translation): 'Do you have a body? Don't sit on the porch. Go out and walk in the rain.'

At the same time, Kabir is only stating half of the case. Nature can even work her way into our fibres when we are simply gazing out of a window. In my mother's house there are several pictures by various artists of someone looking out of a window. Why is it that this should be such a common scene for artists to paint? Thinking in a linear, psychological way, we might suppose that the window separates one from the reality of wind and rain; that the person inside is dreaming of a place or a possibility that they are not yet able to reach. Perhaps; but a room with a view is a place for 'dreamtime'; it can slip one into a world that is not of the physical dimension, and yet which relies on the view from the window for its inspiration. The swaying of branches and the passing of clouds still the daily preoccupations and awaken the deeper imagination, evoking the birth of fresh perceptions and new ideas. This is why the window seats on trains and planes are the first to be filled. Even behind glass the natural world can restore us to our simple and uncluttered nature as nothing else can.

We usually do not even hear the conversation between the instinctual side of our nature and Nature itself; yet it is a constant, though subterranean dialogue. Our intestines and loins and sometimes the heart, are always leaping out to the hills and woodlands we pass through. This was so obvious in earlier times that people personified this exchanging of energy, and heard the trees speaking and the wind crying. In *The Aeneid*, Virgil breaks off a branch and blood comes out, the branch speaks.[14] The soul of the world is under threat from a culture who can no longer hear the voice in the wind. We can no longer afford to stop up our ears and our eyes. If we continue to do so, it is our own soul that will die, not that of the World, which will outlive our threats and go its own way.

Robert Bly

— 10 —
Robert Bly

Robert Bly has been a prominent voice in American poetry since the Vietnam War, when he supported with such elegance the anti-war movement. In the 1980s, however, he has become legendary as the inspiration behind the many men's groups that now exist in the United States. The question of male identity and what constitutes manhood is an important one today. Through myth, storytelling, and the exchange of experiences, Bly has sought to explore the stages and the trials of manhood with groups of men all over the country, as well as in England. It was to hold a men's group that I invited Robert Bly to England on behalf of the Open Gate. I had previously met him at the Ojai Foundation in California, where he was running a workshop for men. What interested me about him was not just that he is a spokesman for men, however. It was also that he is a voice for the spiritual seeker and lover; especially through his renderings of Kabir, but also through many of his poems in the *Loving a Woman in Two Worlds* collection. His words have given voice to my own mad longings, and I wanted to hear his own views on how and where the sacred might be touched upon in a world as secular as ours. The conversation that followed made it clear how Nature and mythology were two of his greatest teachers. After the Open Gate workshop, we met in a hotel in London.

'Well, you know,' he said, 'I lay the sacred between the paws of animals. To me the sacred is connected with the ancient hunting life, and an experience of living that was common before the birth of cities. As far as men are concerned, much of what the sacred points to lies in their ancient link with animals. Joseph Campbell, in *Ways of Animal Powers*, says all gods were originally animals or had an animal form. For women, the sacred, I notice, has roots in the experiences women had with the creation and destruction of life, also before the time of the cities. Now I don't mean there's been nothing sacred since the advent of cities, but I mean to suggest that the word sacred does not only imply divine elevation, or the world of archetypes, or that the sacred arises only as the result of fasting or ritual.'

'Between the paws of animals'. The phrase stirred me, though I felt I had only grasped the surface of its meaning. I asked him to elucidate and he replied by reciting one of his poems in his gruff voice.

On an early morning I think I shall live forever!
I, wrapped in my joyful flesh,
As the grass is wrapped in its clouds of green.

Rising from a bed, where I dreamt
Of long rides past castles and hot coals,
The sun lies happily on my knees;
I have suffered and survived the night
Bathed in dark water, like any blade of grass.

The strong leaves of the box elder tree,
Plunging in the wind, call us to disappear
Into the wilds of the universe,
Where we shall sit at the foot of a plant,
And live forever, like the dust.

'That poem is in my first book, called *Silence and the Snowy Fields*. It was published when I was 36. I'd say that a little experience of the ancient hunter is touched upon there in several lines, particularly the survival like a blade of grass. Also it's a particular place in the universe that is chosen to disappear into – the wild place. Our ancestral chain, as men, starts with the hunter and his instincts and his intimate participation in the natural world about him. This is our heritage. The poem also has a Taoist feeling about it, even though all the details are from an American childhood, and it was written in the Middle West, in Minnesota. It's the Taoist idea that one need not go to a cathedral; the proper object of prayer or devotion is the weed in your backyard.' 'This would be the view of the English Romantics'. I spoke more to myself than to him, but he caught my words.

'Yes, particularly Wordsworth, but not just the English; just as much the Irish medieval poets that Frank O'Connor translated and most of all the German stream, Hoelderlin and Goethe and Novalis. Also, it is the view of Spanish poets like Machado who came partly out of the Arab tradition and partly out of the European. The Arabs find a great deal of the sacred in the feminine, and Taoists certainly consider most grass and trees as feminine.'

'However, most people today don't live surrounded by grass and trees,' I replied. 'If you confine the sacred to a communion with and through Nature, what does that hold out for people in cities?'

Bly responded immediately. 'Wordsworth does not see progress as going from childhood to adolescence to adulthood but as going from childhood to *Nature* to adulthood. Unless a child has that intervening time with Nature, he may never become an adult. I know that's a tough thing to say, that those in the cities may never have a sense of the sacred. There are always exceptions but we mustn't imagine that what is sacred can emerge or appear no matter how life is lived.'

'But Wordsworth, and you too, in your poem, evoked a picture of the imagination, not just a physical connection with Nature. Surely the realm of the imagination is available anywhere, in cities or on mountains?'

'Wordsworth says not. I know this is very unfashionable material I am presenting here, but my certainty derives from the idea that the imagination is a power, like the spiritual intellect, which rises from unknown sources and has the power of a great thunderstorm. Imagination requires food, as a horse does, and contrary to many Jungian speculations, the food of the imagination is not archetypes, but the actual energy given off by old tree roots, mountains, rocks, glaciers, fields of barley, crows. It's a rather radical idea. We could say that when English and French people in the eighteenth century suddenly began to experience the Alps as sublime, it didn't mean only that a new way of looking had happened to the painters but that the European body had opened itself in some mysterious way to the actual energy discharges coming from mountains and rivers. We notice it in Turner. Turner's body did not pick up remarkable radiations from human beings. I saw the Turner collection today and notes said that he was notoriously neglectful of his family. The people and faces in Turner, unlike those in Rembrandt, are not usually carefully delineated. They're just figures. But he received some kind of massive infusion from the ocean and land-scapes. He felt it in the Italian countryside, and apparently every time he got out on to the ocean. I am suggesting, then, that the European body was able to open itself to food arriving by invisible means.'

I paused for a moment. What Robert had just said had reminded me of Mount Athos again; of walking along a cliff path in the late afternoon and suddenly realising that although I had not eaten since the night before I was not in the slightest bit hungry. I could feel my body being fed by the sea, the sky and the rocks in a way that made ordinary food seem irrelevant. I asked Robert whether he felt that this Romantic sensitivity of the European spirit was re-awakening now, with the return to Nature of the 1960s and the growing ecological awareness of the 1980s. He questioned my word 'spirit' immediately.

'You know, I take seriously the ancient distinction of soul and spirit. According to the ancients, spirit is male in tone, associated with fire, and it ascends. Soul is feminine in tone, associated with water, and it descends. Actual men and women, of course, are both soul and spirit. Some women have more spirit than men, and some men have more soul than women. So I would say that we are talking here about a movement of soul, not of spirit. Yes, I do think there's been a deepening of soul in the last decades, more and more descent into soul. The "New Age" is continually looking for spirit when actually what is happening is a movement down into soul. Hillman said an interesting thing – that the danger in spirit now is that it is contaminated with victory. A white St Michael kills the dark Water-Dragon. It could be described as spirit killing soul. We know that in one Palestinian version of the story, which the Crusaders picked up there, the Dragon when defeated turns into a young woman. In that version, spirit, by attacking and engaging with soul, is able to allow soul to turn into a human form, a female human form. That is a very different story than the one we get in which the Dragon dies. The West tends to insist that spirit be victorious over both body and soul, or over both earth and water. Soul, then,' he continued, 'lives among and becomes the defeated, as it lives among the blacks in America, who have a great deal of soul. However, I believe that soul is becoming more vigorous everywhere in the West. The movements you just mentioned, for example, are movements of the souls of men and women to protect the Earth. It isn't the mind that protects the Earth – mind scorns the Earth. We could say that the community is trying to stop killing the Earth Dragon. The community seems to have made a decision. Maybe it has even taken away St Michael's horse.'

Suddenly connections began to form in my mind. 'What that distinction reminded me of,' I said, 'between spirit and soul, is the distinction you make in men's groups between the need for men to find their feminine and the necessity for men to find the deep masculine. It seems to me, too, that what we're not in touch with is true spirit, which might for men be connected with what you call the deep masculine. What has masqueraded as spirit for centuries now is mind, which of course is not spirit at all. In fact this association of mind with spirit is I am sure a major reason for the spirit's impoverishment.'

'Yes,' Bly replied. 'The practical mind is so powerful now that it has contaminated spirit. I do think that the phrase "the deep masculine" implies also deeper levels of soul. There is an inwardness in the masculine psyche which amounts to a union of soul and spirit at a very deep level. Most of us are not in touch with it. The gods we have venerated for the last two thousand years do not include Dionysius, who represented for men and women a deep union of soul and spirit, associated with tearing and being torn apart. We humans are less and less aware of the kind of tearing that Nature does in its own being – for example the way kernels of corn are torn away from the cob in order to be planted. These metaphors used to be deeply reassuring to humans. But what is torn away in the city is almost never put back together again. Contemporary people no longer see the normal acts of Nature such as the fox chasing her cubs out of the nest in autumn or the way wine-makers tear grapes away from the mother vine. I think that the absence of these assuring memories in the psyche results in people being paralysed at the instant they need to be torn. Men aren't confident that they can be torn apart and put back together again. Another way to put that is that contemporary men are afraid of grief.'

His last remark struck a chord in me. 'Yes,' I said, 'the myth of the hero still lives on. It isn't easy to generate new myths, is it?'

Robert Bly laughed. 'People used to go to Joseph Campbell and say, "Mr Campbell, these are very interesting old myths you are telling us, but I want to create my own myth." "Well, that's good," Joseph would say. "I hope for your sake that you live 10,000 years because that's how long it takes to create a myth." A young woman came up to him in California after a typical Campbell lecture in which he had presented something like 40,000 years of transformation and grief in an hour and a half. One's mind is so stunned by the magnitude of it all that it can hardly right itself afterwards. The young woman spoke to him and remarked, "I found that very interesting, Mr Campbell, but I think people my age don't have to go through all that any more." "Oh. Why is that?" he asked. "Because there is so much spiritual material available to us now that we can go directly from youth to wisdom." Joseph replied, "Oh, that's wonderful, my dear. All you've missed is life!"'

'So life in this case,' Robert continued, 'is trouble and the recognition that you can't make a new myth. You live in a constant struggle with the old myths, trying to separate some of your life out from the old patterns and then seeing your life swallowed by them again and again, and once more fighting to come back and establish something individual. Joseph Campbell used to say that one reason to study fairy tales and myths is to find out which myth you are living. After you have studied that for twenty years, you might ask which myth is living you. In saying this he was pointing to the ancient idea that the divine lives human beings, not the other way around.'

'We have spoken of Nature as a help,' I said, 'but what other forces can assist in the awakening of soul?'

'Well, I myself feel that sound is very powerful. Sound is much older than we are. The Koran is a sound-book. Then one must mention meditation, ritual, and dance, all of which work best in cultures where the person is already grounded in Nature. Then, I think that mythology keeps soul alive when wakened. Kerenyi says that mythology for variety, intensity, abundance, and grandeur can only be compared with Nature itself. It has an awesome power to enliven.'

'Yes, and yet the young lady who asked the question of Joseph Campbell is typical. Two or three people asked similar questions in your workshop this weekend. We are not familiar with mythology today. We no longer have an oral tradition, and mythology was never meant to be something we read about in books. I suppose psychotherapy is the most available means for people today to touch the mythology that lives them.'

'Well, it is and it isn't,' Bly replied. 'I see a movement from ethical thinking to psychological thinking taking place around 1899, and a movement in this present decade from psychological thinking to mythological thinking. The mythical is not behind us but ahead of us. At the same time we could never have entered it, or re-entered it, without the superb psychologists who have lived and written since 1899. Let me tell you another idea I heard from Joseph Campbell. We know that animals perform certain actions, such as nest building, instinctually. Solutions they have worked out in the past that encourage their survival are preserved inside through what we call instincts. If the nest is torn down the bird builds another. It knows certain songs instinctually. It is interesting to note that if a bird's song is interrupted it must go back to the beginning and start again. Instincts, then, result in non-spontaneous behaviour. It was decided, however, that human beings need tremendous openness of response, so they could react to sudden changes of climate and environment, or to new animal enemies or new neighbours. The information that is helpful for their survival is stored, not inside, as it is for animals, but outside, in myths and fairy stories. That is an amazing idea. Old men and women used to remember stories exactly, word by word, because that is where the culture's knowledge was stored, and their survival depended upon it.'

Bly was really moving into his stride. 'It is amazing,' he continued, 'to think that the stories preserved by the Grimm Brothers, by the Sufis, by the ancient Greeks, are granaries or storehouses on the outside of the human brain. In a sense, we don't need new ideas now, we need the knowledge that can be found in our storehouses. That is why mythology is appropriate and even essential in this latter part of the century.'

I then asked him what he felt were the collective myths at work in our culture at present.

'I have spoken of the value of the "Iron John" myth for men, in which we find the Wild Man lying at the bottom of the male psyche "under the water". I am just finishing a book on that story. Then, for both men and women, I think Snow White is important,' Bly added, causing me some surprise. 'The young feminine is being damaged throughout our culture. Robert Johnson remarked the other day that he was more and more convinced that whenever an advance in consciousness takes place, it is the young feminine that has to pay. When Hamlet makes an advance in consciousness, Ophelia is one of the first to pay – she goes mad and drowns. When a family leaves the country for the city, in South America, in China, in India – it is the "young feminine", whether in men or in women, who pays. The young feminine needs the protection and the stability of Nature.

Another way to put it is that when a mathematical genius, let's say, gains a lot of consciousness, he puts the young feminine in himself at risk. It would be her joy, her enthusiasm for life, her ability to feel, that would suffer. Outwardly, young women take the wound. Some of the suffering behind the women's movement has been brought about by technological culture and "computer consciousness".

'So Snow White,' Bly went on, 'says that when the young feminine suffers damage it will go to the dwarves. They are beings of imagination connected to earth below and – through the seven minerals – to the planets above. So the young feminine goes downward into the earth and upward into the heavens for protection, in a way abandoning the surface of the earth. She goes to *matter* for help, although in a way that proves not to be sufficient – she falls into a sleep and lies in a glass coffin for years. That myth says that the feminine needs healing; and that only the "dwarves" and a good connection to matter can do that. The story says that the young feminine isn't entirely able to wake up. There was a sense in the early Renaissance the feminine was awake – Botticelli's *Spring* is an example, and the Mona Lisa – all these vibrant, alive feminine faces of the Renaissance. All that has changed. For example, when I visit a poetry workshop in the States and people there show me their poems, I find that among the women, two out of three poems will have images of dismemberment, sometimes from actual dreams. Horrendous images are coming through the poems of young women. I don't think that is personal to them. The feminine inside the young men has suffered dismemberment as well.

'Now,' Robert went on, 'let's return to our story. We know that no fairy story ends in actual marriage: the beings inside a story are inside a single soul. The story says that Snow White wakes up at last when she accepts a connection with her own interior male. She needs to be in the mood of a lover when she accepts that "kiss". That, however, is complicated. Some women are warriors now to protect themselves. Does that prevent the subtle transformation of the "kiss" from happening? Probably.'

'What of the myth of the hero,' I asked, 'the dynamo of the whole Protestant ethic? Surely this is still at the heart of our culture?'

'Probably so, but the hero myth for men is just one of the many, many myths, and it has been vastly overemphasised.

St George is not much use any more. Men need the myths of defeat, such as Dionysius, who was eaten by the Titans. Defeat became vivid for American men in Vietnam, and the Russians have experienced it in Afghanistan. Gorbachev understands the myths of defeat; Bush does not. The myths to come will be very old. They will be sobering in the view they give us of ourselves. It will be the dragon's view.'

'How is it possible for us to recapture, to reconnect again with mythological thinking?'

'We would stop saying "our God was born in Bethlehem". The Divine is never born at any one time or place. It is not "our God", either. Mythological feeling asks you to imagine a divine world entirely independent of time or space, and mythological thinking asks you to understand that the Divine is born inside our own bodies by virgin birth each time we speak truth from the heart.

'I'll come back to that in a moment. James Hillman says something very helpful about mythological imagination. In such imagination, everything happens in pairs. To have a story you can't have Zeus alone, you need Zeus *and* Hera; you need Jesus *and* Mary Magdelene, Radha *and* Krishna. You have Great Father *and* Great Mother to contend with. It was the Great Mother who poisoned Snow White in the end. Psychology allows you to concentrate on one complex at a time. Mythology doesn't allow that because our life is a story.

'Now, to return to what I was saying. In mythology events do not take place in Jerusalem but inside the body. Blake said as much, and he is the master of mythological thinking in England:

> I shall not rest from mental fight
> Nor shall my sword sleep in my hand
> Til we have built Jerusalem
> In England's green and pleasant land.

'He means that we have to keep thinking and imagining until "Jerusalem" is felt inside each English man and woman. Finally, I would say that if the mood of ethical or fundamentalist thinking is blame and punishment and the mood of psychological thinking is humour and forgiveness, then the essence of mythological thinking is gratitude for immense abundance. The abundance in the soul resembles the stars at night. Blake said, "What we call the body is only the portion of soul discerned by the five senses."'

Robert Bly sat back in his chair. 'But these aren't complete answers by any means,' he said, as we came to the end of our talk. 'How do I know? You will have to ask me again in a few years.'

Intimate Relationship

'A Third Body'

A man and a woman sit near each other, and they do
   not long
at this moment to be older, or younger, nor born
in any other nation, or time, or place,
They are content to be where they are, talking or
   not talking.
Their breaths together feed someone whom we do not
   know.
The man sees the way his fingers move;
he sees her hands close around a book she hands to
   him.
They obey a third body that they share in common.
They have made a promise to love that body.
Age may come, parting may come, death will come.
A man and a woman sit near each other;
as they breathe they feed someone we do not know,
someone we know of, whom we have never seen. [15]

For one human being to love another, that is the
ultimate, the last test and proof, the work for which all
other work is but a preparation.

(Rainer Maria Rilke)

One can only arrive at the experience of Robert Bly's poem,
the presence of the third body, through a mysterious
alchemy of effort and grace. One has to make room in oneself
for such intimacy to occur, and yet it can never be on call, or
at one's command. Intimacy lies beyond the limits of the
strategic mind. What follows, then, rather than any strategy,

is a personal account of intimacy, as I know it with the person I share my life with.

Like most of us, I have not always found relationship easy. It has most often presented itself as a living paradox. I shall never forget being out on a walk as a student at university and suddenly realising how much I enjoyed life on my own and in my own company, after having been in a relationship for a while; and yet noticing *at the same time* how part of my being was wanting to be drawn back into relationship again.

Today, as ever, these two aspects of myself and the interaction between them constitute a major theme in my experience of relationship. The love of aloneness is first of all the need to feel oneself, to have time and space to give intimacy to one's own thoughts, feelings and sensations. This feeling of oneself descends in a tangible, almost physical way, with a renewed awareness of one's psychic field and ground. Deeper still, it is a contact with, and ultimately an identification with, a silence and presence that seems to regard both oneself and others with a compassionate detachment. I suspect that Jacob Needleman is correct when he suggests in his book, *Lost Christianity*, that what people long for first and foremost is not contact with some divine Otherness, but with self, the individual sense of being that can say I am – not this, or that, but simply that I am here. This here, this closeness to oneself, seems to me to be the wellspring of all ideas and feelings that might be deemed creative, that take me beyond my ordinary, habitual activity and thinking. Certainly, some of the most creative activities I engage in – writing, thinking, dreaming, meditating – take place when I am alone. It is not surprising then that when this feeling of self-ness arises, it moves me to want to place myself in a situation where more of the same can ensue.

It may seem strange to begin a chapter on relationship in praise of solitude. Yet surely the one of necessity evokes the other. It is because of the counter-balance of relationship that I can experience my solitude in a way that need not be withdrawal, but a creative process of respiration. It is because of the experience of my own self that I can know in relationship a unity in which I do not dissolve, but am part of a life, a world, that is larger than the confines of my own skin and my own stream of thoughts and feelings.

It is not only the relief of being in intimate contact again with one's own inner world that emerges from being alone. Relationship itself can become *more* conscious, in certain ways, when one is not immersed in its daily actuality. I am usually aware, for example, of a general undercurrent of connectedness, an intuition of my partner's intimate presence – not in the realm of thought or feeling, but in an energetic realm – wherever I may be, and whoever I may or may not be with. Her presence feels closer to me than my own body, mingled in with my very lifestream in a way that makes the awareness of her and of I almost indistinguishable. I have often wondered how the presence of God might enter me in a similar way. I do not seek to have this feeling; it is there as a given, as it were, of our knowing each other, and in my partner's absence it quickly flows close to the surface. Absence, then, is an essential feature of intimate relationship for me; a condition that, like the night, gives birth to secret things; that gives a depth and a tangible poignancy to what in the light of daily company are fleeting intimations that the mind's breath can rarely give voice to.

Why, though, is it often so difficult to have the sensation of being close to oneself when in the company of the other? It is not the company itself which is the difficulty so much as where one's attention is when in company. If I am out walking with my partner, or sitting in relative silence – if we are doing anything that encourages our natural being to emerge, then, since we both share the common wish for it, that inner silence and simple collectedness can arise even more substantially than when I am alone. However, in sharing one's life with someone, one is also sharing the everyday obligations of survival and social interaction with the world in general.

These necessities evoke the social self, the personality, which siphons attention away from the prior sensation of oneself that can be felt in simple moments. We do not usually have the inner force of stabilised attention required to maintain that sensation of ourselves at the same time as being in the everyday world of needs and desires. Such a connection does occur at times, but the great majority of our daily life of relationship is spent within the domain of the personality. It is from our own personality then, which is brought into play through everyday relationships, that we need space and solitude, rather than from our partner. However, one of the potentials of relationship is precisely that it can be the arena in which these two forces of personality and of stabilised inner attention can be brought together.

What kind of relationship can there be if much of our existence is spent in the realm of the personality with its fears and its hopes, its ambitions and its needs? This is the very drama that relationship is presumed to consist of. Two fears I have been aware of are the loss of freedom (that is, the fear of responsibility and limit) and the fear of not being sufficiently stretched or challenged – of not continually exploring new ground, of being stuck in the habitual round of mechanical response patterns. These anxieties are normally an integral part of intimate relationship itself. They have provided shadow and contrast to all that I know of intimacy, and they have offered a door to a deeper and humbler sense of my own condition.

The fear of responsibility and limit would appear most plainly when I turned my head to look at another woman. In this there was at times a natural vibrancy, and at times straightforward lust. All I could do in such a moment was to attempt to experience the tension of neither repressing the impulse nor acting upon it. What I have tried to do is enter into contact with my own bodily sensations without judgement; and/or consciously praise the flow of life through the instincts, seeing it as a gift of aliveness. Or, I would forget all the above and experience the dullness and frustration of titillation or flirtation. It was not a question of being dissatisfied or unfulfilled by my own relationship, and of my eyes constantly roving elsewhere. If that had been the case, I would not have been long in following my instincts. No, on the contrary, I have always been fulfilled with my partner in every way. The whole matter is far, far more ancient than this. It may even have been, in fact, that my head turned precisely because I recognised the fullness of our intimacy and was engaging in a last stand for the imagined freedom of unattachment. Perhaps. I do not know. It serves less to give an answer than to lean into the question by gazing honestly into my actual experience.

In a literal sense our relationship is a monogamous one – not out of social morality, nor the wish to pander to each other's fears and jealousies, nor because of a ruling we have made. It is so because it is fitting. In another way it is both monogamous and open. It is a container that is open to the world but it remains nevertheless a container which derives strength and substance from its own shape and limits. We both intuit that these limits are important in helping us to experience, to feel ourselves with a closeness that would not be present if we had no boundaries. How else could I know my own fear of confinement, which itself is a contradiction stretching deep into the recesses of my own psyche and of the collective itself? Relationship conceived as a context for self-knowledge and for a deeper opening to life starts right here, with the eyes and ears of the heart up against the face of this fundamental and primary recoil.

The fear of not continually exploring new ground, of being subject to the mediocrity of the habitual and the familiar, is another face of the same contraction. I remember an evening several months after we first met when my partner, on impulse, made dinner for us in her flat. We had been to restaurants often, but neither of us had ever made a meal for the other before. As we sat down at the table our eyes met and we were both instantly aware that we were enacting the eternal ritual that men and women do with each other all over the world every day, in straw huts, in suburbia, and in great mansions. Woman prepares meal, man and woman sit down at table. At the same moment, without a word needing to be spoken, we both experienced this simple activity as a great weight, a yoke that bound us to the countless millions who sat down together day after day, enveloped in the mediocrity of the daily round. Neither of us were able to pick up a fork for minutes on end, and though there was something utterly comical about it, we were literally held in the gravity of the experience.

This fear is of my own ordinariness, my own mediocrity and feet of clay. It registers as boredom, lassitude and restlessness. It is a sense of my own limits, my own dullness and lack of creative vision; a feeling that I am going nowhere and that I have done nothing. The awareness of my ordinary mortality is painful indeed for the one in me who aspires to immortality, who wants to make a mark that future genera- tions will speak of; and yet who, like most mortals, has no special gifts to commend him and who is bound to the wheel of the daily humdrum round. Life with another inevitably engenders this fear, for our plainness is easy to see in the mirror of a shared existence.

Then, our life together naturally gathers habits and rituals that are more evident for their sharing – habits of speech, of touch, of call and response, of interaction in general, but especially habits of seeing.

Despite ourselves, despite our capacity to see and taste the wellspring that is always revealing the other and our re- lationship as new, our eyes will still tend, out of habit and lack of vigilance – out of the dust of our ordinary humanness – to condense images of the other that are convenient half- truths, sketches etched in the imagination that reassure us we know who we are living with. I am only gradually recognising the essential value of the dust in our eyes and our feet of clay. Our poverty is part of our truth; it is part of our offering to each other, we who are not angels. Our ordinary imperfections are the doorways to a certain intima- tion of the nature of love. Listen to Robert Bly, in this extract from his poem, 'Listening to the Köln Concert':

When men and women come together,
How much they have to abandon! Wrens
make their nests of fancy threads
and string ends, animals

abandon all their money each year.
What is it that men and women leave?
Harder than wren's doing, they have
to abandon their longing for the perfect.

The inner nest not made by instinct
will never be quite round,
and each has to enter the nest
made by the other imperfect bird.

The awareness of our interior poverty and the admission of
it is itself a kind of grace, whose touch is by no means felt
with reliable frequency. More common is the absorption in
the mechanical demands of daily living. Everyday necessities
gobble up time so that we find it no easy thing to retain a
portion of the day or night simply to be with each other in a
way that might intentionally water the soul. We pass each
other running up and down the stairs, we call out pieces of
information to each other, we ruminate over future projects
and financial necessities, and if one of us is not on the
telephone then the other is. Outwardly, it is in the engine
room of our mutual projects that we most frequently enter
into contact. Certainly we share whatever excitement and
interest arises from our various initiatives, but often our
communication is concrete, factual and cursory. Sometimes
we exchange knowing glances as we pass each other
going in or out of a room, or over a brief cup of coffee,
knowing that we are each on the move in our own world and
that is how it needs to be – how we need it to be, since we are
the creators of all the movement.

One way we have of slipping under our mechanical
natures and their habitual patterns is to fall into silence. We
sit in silent meditation daily; then there is the silence that
falls on a meal, or on a train journey, or sitting watching the
clouds through the window. Apart from meditation, the
most exquisite silence for me is that in which I am simply
resting with the other, without any impulse to do anything,
or make anything of it, or lead it in any direction. The current
of connectedness that I have already mentioned can then
make itself felt, and can join a larger circuit that gathers
everything into its orbit. In this silence one can hear the one
life breathing. Any sense of my own uniqueness or special-
ness dissolves away and we are both simply there, invisible
somehow, and present at the same time. What will chase this

intimacy away, or prevent it taking form in the first place, is self-consciousness, or the attempt to 'engage' in relationship, or simple impatience. There are lesser forms of silence that also have their place, such as that which falls after a period of intense talking, or which is there just because there is nothing to say while one is doing the washing-up or driving down the motorway. Whereas the first silence has an ordinariness which is also a fullness, in a three-dimensional way, these last are ordinary in a slacker, humbler manner.

It may seem from the previous few paragraphs that we are either in silence or exchanging cursory comments on the stairs about business. Surreptitiously, almost as if through sleight of hand, the chiselling of experience into language gives actuality another turn and appears to move it in directions that it can barely recognise. In fact, we pass many words back and forth between us that are the carriers of our enthusiasm, our laughter, our seeking, and our longing. Speech, the very faculty which can deaden a relationship and preclude any hope of intimacy whatsoever, is at the same time that which can give power and form to the inarticulate whisperings of the heart – to that centre in oneself which has its own authority and affiliation with a deeper lifestream. Words seem so available that it may appear of no significance that we use them automatically and even exclusively as stop-gaps, throw-aways, diminutives or vituperatives, or like the mechanical utterances of computer ticker tape.

Yet it does matter; we have a responsibility, especially with the one we live with, to use the power of speech as a bearer of truth, warmth, beauty and respect – as a vehicle for that which moves and awakens us. How I address the person I live with matters; the tone and weight of my voice has its impact, the nature and subject of our conversation will leave its trace. My words often betray me; they lay bare my inauthenticity, my shallowness and harshness, my sloppy and peremptory nature. But I know, too, their capacity for commun-ing, connection, engagement. We slip words into each other that light up our mutual excitements and con-cerns. Through words we impart to each other our deepest, barely audible responses to the immensity of life. Faced with the automaticity of our ordinary minds, however, and our general lack of discipline and attention, we find it necessary – invaluable even – to take half an hour most days to make our speaking more conscious. We sit facing each other and are attentive while we each in turn speak on our relationship, on our feelings for each other and for life, and on anything we may have been holding back from the other. In this way we encourage each other to use speech as a vehicle for truth.

Sometimes, though, the more inarticulate we are the closer we are to ourselves and to each other: the times when, for example, I experience what I can only describe as a delight in the company of my partner. I mean by this a subtle thing, not some unbridled effervescence that dissipates itself through exaggerated gesture or speech. It can ripple outward in laughter, in a sigh, or in some soft, unintelligible sound, at times with a gesture of the hand or inclining of the head.

Sounds lend themselves naturally to being joined with in chorus; words, however, are spoken to be listened to. Listening is one of the subtlest, most profound means of communication available to us. Occasionally, I catch myself hearing my partner in a way that reminds me I barely know what listening is. I hear the timbre of her voice, and through it, the weight and pitch of her being, the unspoken words that accompany her speech, and the very movement of her nerves and blood. To listen in this way is to receive the person into one's very body; it is an activity not of the ear but of the entire organism. This listening effects what I can only describe as an alchemical change in both parties, through which both are opened and revealed, to themselves and to each other, and through which a deep mixing and mingling of being takes place. It may arise spontaneously in response to the other's words, to the authenticity and presence they convey; as a moment of unsolicited grace; or through the force of one's own intention and attention, the mark of one's wish fully to receive and honour one's partner.

This is a gift I am able to offer only in rare moments. For the most part, the space around me is too full of my own preoccupations, opinions and prejudices to be able to hear any more than the first layers of her speech; and the wish in me is simply not strong enough most of the time to engender the silent and spacious presence that can give rise to this depth of listening. Nevertheless it occurs, and reminds me with acuteness of what is possible and what is normally the case. There is as well the listening not to words but to whom a person really is and what it is they really need. This is a lifelong labour of love which I have barely embarked upon at all.

Touching is as deceptively available as listening. The two of us are touched by each other all the time – around the head, the hands, the face, shoulders, everywhere. Our bodies and limbs fold round each other naturally and easily. Our touching is the carrier of our enjoyment and delight in the other, of our desire sometimes, or our caring, of our support and upholding, of our recognition that the other is there. And sometimes it is the mechanical grasp with which one ordinarily handles an object, a grasp without contact, oblivious of the life that is coursing beneath the hand.

There have been times when touch has led us into the awe and wonder of what it is to be human. One hand placed anywhere on the other's body long enough and still enough can pass through layer upon layer of deepening contact. It is as if in the stillness and the silence the body can render up its resistances, its unconscious tensions and withholdings, and give way to the emergence of a true tenderness, a quality that is not an emotion but an open-handed communion with the other. There is no attempt to enter into communion; rather the starting point is where we are, perhaps in a relative absence of feeling contact. It is a matter of simply being there, abiding there. And yet, and yet, in this availability is a willing attention; and it is this which can guide us, as if following a scent, through the open door of touch to the deeper reaches of ourselves. There have been occasions when our limbs have merged to the degree that we have literally been unable to be sure what belonged to who, or to separate ourselves from the field that contained us. Touch, touching, being touched, can generate the deepest respect for the mystery and the magnitude of power inherent in the simplest and smallest of acts.

Making love is the encapsulation, the gathering together, of everything I have already described. In fact, speaking, silence, listening, touching, and even the absence of the other, are all different forms of making love, in the sense of the interpenetration of personal energy and in the sense, too, of being taken up as one breath into a state of presence that is greater and more than simply the sum of the two of us. I have rarely known a time when the physical act of making love with my partner did not incorporate both these levels. It is an act of surrender and an act of strength; of vigour and infinite tenderness; of listening, of silence, and of speaking; of surprise, astonishment even, and unpredictability; of tears, of laughter, and of deep rest; of the dark, instinctual forces of our mysterious, carnal nature, and the radiance of That which breathes us all. It is, of all acts, the act in which we may stand revealed.

My partner is not only my lover in the sense of being the one with whom I most fully express the eros of desire, joy, energy and laughter; she is also my sister, my brother and friend, with whom I share the love of companionship along the path of life. Often I feel us to be the same gender, neither male nor female, but two human beings who are stirred by the same longing for Life itself. The love of – the turning towards, the feeling called by – the current of Life that stands behind all life, is the love in which we are most deeply united. It is here that we are most intimate of all, for in this common turning we share the deepest, the stillest, and also the most ardent of what we know life to be. It is from the same well that we drink the essential meaning of our life.

Does this mean, though, that this relationship is necessarily a context for spiritual practice? And what do I mean by 'spiritual', and by the images of 'the well we both share' and 'the Presence that lives and breathes us'? These are all personal turns of phrase for a universal known by many names. Do I mean some vague entity that floats in and out of our awareness? Do I mean an entity at all, either interior to me or exterior? No, I mean rather a tangible aliveness which permeates all and which is itself somehow awake, conscious, compassionate, neither within me nor without me, neither with form nor without form, known in and through the body but not in any way restricted to it. What feels to be my fuller humanity awakens in and as this Presence – my body is alive and still, as is my mind; awe, wonder, substantiality, gathered attention, purposeful availability, silence – any or all of these may make themselves known. Now we both know this dimension of our human condition and we share similar language to describe it. The knowledge of it informs our relationship with a particular tone that steers us from the beginning in its direction. It provides a fertile ground, but the labour of the tilling remains to be done. In fact our shared predisposition can even make any genuine practice more difficult by shrouding the relationship in some false sense of spiritual security, some illusion of innate spiritual accomplishment or grace.

If relationship as a practice is to mean anything we cannot afford to rest in the realm of subtle delight. The practice lies in deepening the attention I have referred to in all the various areas of our meeting in such a way as to bring before us the awareness both of who we are on a daily basis and who we can be in our fulness. It is the gradual fastening of our remembrance on the current that is both in and independent of all forms, including the relationship itself.

Relationship is the way of the lover; it is the way which is ultimately without technique, in which a progressively steady and transparent gaze can enter the mystery of the other and of the relationship itself and fall on the empty mirror beyond all form. It is a way of rigour, of fire, of tears and song. If it is alive it responds not to patterns of fear and habit but to what is fitting; accordingly it might change shape at any moment, or, might even seem to disappear altogether. Yet, like any true way it is, once fully bitten, a way of no escape; for once two wills have co-mingled into one, something is formed that outlives all arrivals and departures or beginnings and endings.

Chlöe Goodchild

— 12 —

Chlöe Goodchild

The previous chapter is only one half – my half – of a shared story. It would not be complete without the view of Chlöe, the person with whom I share my life. After reading what I had to say on our relationship, her first comment was that she, as a woman, would approach some of the same themes from a rather different perspective. The question I first raised, for example – the need for creative aloneness – she saw to be one of the major challenges for a woman in relationship today. This was hardly surprising. As well as being a mother and in relationship with me, Chlöe runs a full-time project called The Inner Voice, in which she runs retreats and courses to encourage people to hear their own inner call. We sat down one evening to discuss these questions from her point of view.

'Like you,' Chlöe said, 'the experience of my own aloneness is fundamental to my appreciating our shared existence together. However, for a woman, it is not always so simple to distinguish individuality from relationship. Traditionally, after all, woman is defined in terms of relationship, in which her primary function is to fulfil her family's domestic needs. Man, on the other hand, is usually defined in terms of his work in the world, and his individual achievements. With this background, it is not difficult to see why the whole question of time to themselves, and individual creativity, is such a significant theme for many women. Having been in a marriage in which these roles were quite strongly present, even though implicitly, I realise how important it is for you and me to question these traditional assumptions and explore new ground.

'I do not mean by this to undermine the essential value of the serving and supporting role of woman – on the contrary, a mutual attitude of service towards the other is fundamental to my view of relationship – especially if we see intimate relationship as a context for spiritual practice. What I am questioning is the way men and women collude in a dynamic that can result in the woman foregoing her own creativity and individuality for the apparent sake and support of her husband. Now I value my own creative work and time to myself as highly as you do, but I have not always found it so easy as you to define my boundaries and to be single-minded in the fulfilment of my own needs. This concern for the welfare of others is obviously a genuine quality that women share, but it can easily work against them. I certainly believe that you and I are learning to serve each other in a more creative way, not least because we share that as a part of our overall purpose in being together. The more we both stand in the ground of our own being, the more we can be a support for each other. It is a two-way process.'

Chlöe went on to point out that there were no clear maps for her to be a woman in the way she found herself being one, either in relationship or in the development of her own work.

'In fact,' she continued, 'it is a primary concern not just for us but for our time to discover what it now means to be truly feminine or truly masculine. For women, to be feminine has traditionally meant to be available and receptive to man's needs – to be able to please, to attract, to behave, and so on. As we know, this has generated the opposite reaction over the last decade or so, as women have struggled to find themselves. The true challenge, though, is to integrate all the various qualities of the feminine, rather than to claim this one to be true and that one to be false. In fact, I believe multiplicity and inclusiveness to be inherent characteristics of the feminine consciousness now emerging in both men and women. In the case of women, among the many archetypal qualities that act on us are, for example, the nun, the lover, the witch and the mother. Our challenge is to re-affirm the positive attributes of all these archetypes, and others besides, and to be any or all of them as life requires. Among the positive attributes of the witch, for example, are her capacity to transform and to heal. The point is that the feminine power that guards the hearth, such as the goddess Hestia, or that sustains the husband, such as Hera, the wife of Zeus, is just one among various feminine qualities.'

I asked Chlöe to expand on what she saw to be the emerging feminine consciousness.

'Well, we have to be careful,' she replied, 'to see that we are talking symbolically. The feminine is not just in women, it is a current that runs throughout humanity. It is in women, though, that it rises more naturally to consciousness. My sense of it is that the feminine has something to do with the consciousness of the borderline. It stands between worlds and is able to see both ways at once. The negative aspect of this might be the inability to make concrete decisions; the positive attribute is the gift of being able to fuse one world with another, to transform opposing forces into a dynamic unity. So, instead of the traditional divisions of either/or, high/low, good/bad, divide and rule, the feminine sees the case for both/and. This can lead to the whole theme of co-operation, which is impinging upon many levels of our society at present. Essentially, the feminine tends to dissolve borders at all levels, from the personal to the global. Look, for example, at what is currently happening in Eastern Europe.

'The power of transformation is a key element of the feminine,' she continued. 'I have already mentioned the witch in this respect, but the transforming power of the lover is another example. Sexual love can bring together the physical and the divine. For man, it offers the eradication of the fear of darkness. The woman can become the dark cave and her clarity and strength can transform man's fear into the experience of union. For both men and women sexual love provides the closest earthly reflection of abandonment into The One. This abandonment, though, is beyond physical orgasm, for in its presence, the flower is constantly open in ecstasy.'

I wanted to know in which other ways Chlöe saw herself to

be bringing the feminine into the intimacy of our relationship. She was silent for a moment.

'I believe,' she said thoughtfully, 'that I help us to appreciate life in a way that is more consciously receptive and cooperative. Traditionally, the power of women has been expressed through conciliation. What we are being called to enact now, however, is the power of conciliation *with* and *through* understanding, or wisdom. This, if you like, is the expression of Sophia – harmony through wisdom, or insight. The authority of Sophia is not confrontational, yet it restores our inner world to order.'

'Another way the feminine enters our relationship,' she continued, 'has to do with space – allowing space for new and unexpected processes to arise – as, for example, when we ensure that we have a certain quality of time with each other. The space we give for intentional contact, as in our relationship exercise that you mentioned in your chapter, allows our communication to become more conscious and our relationship to breathe.

'Then there is that quality of the mother, when one or both of us is truly being of service to the other. I am speaking here of service at a profound level, the level of having an unconditional regard for the other, supporting them in who they are. This, we might call the eventual, or ultimate aim of any relationship considered as spiritual practice. The true feminine also has something to do with inspiration for me, particularly in relation to music, song and celebration.'

Chlöe paused for a moment, and then continued.

'Again,' she said, 'if we take the realm of work, how might the response of the feminine archetype differ from that of the masculine? Your paradigm in relation to work, for example, is more of a hierarchical one. My model tends rather to the decentralised picture. I derive more satisfaction from being part of a group in which leadership skills and responsibility are shared. We might say yours is more a vertical, mine a horizontal, model. Both have their value, but when they come up against each other in one of our joint projects, we can sometimes find ourselves in a battle of wills. What we are really engaging in is a new form of relationship, in which subservience and domination are replaced by a shared creative dynamic. I, for my part,' she went on, 'impede that when I lose my boundaries, by endeavouring to become "over-cooperative" and "helpful". You, I think, obstruct it when you make your boundaries too defined and rigid. Boundaries, leadership issues, and·competitiveness all challenge our *ideals* of relationship and bring us face to face with the actuality of it. This is another feature of the feminine consciousness – it is not afraid of ideals being tested in the forge of everyday humdrum existence, with all the uncertainty and even confusion that may imply.'

At this point I asked Chlöe what this new pattern of relationship was that she felt we were working towards. She smiled.

'Eventually,' she replied, 'we are working towards the elimination of suffering. What that means for the present is the practice of the creative dynamic I was speaking about just now. It also means the practice of "no blame". A fundamental belief that most of us have, although often unconsciously, is that the other person can give us what we want, which is happiness. In other words, we easily harbour the notion that our partner is the one who is our ideal, the one who can "save" us, or vice versa. This inevitably leads to disappointment and eventually to disillusionment. The disillusionment is all the stronger if, as is usually the case, we try to fit our partner into our own story-line, so that they will play the part we want. Given that concrete images, or story-lines, inevitably arise in us all in regard to others, you and I share the task of acknowledging our story-lines as we see them arise, without blaming ourselves or each other. The way we can wake up to these story-lines is through creative friction. When this is really happening, it is like an edge that we walk together, which is grounded in openness – in an attitude of willing inquiry. Inquiry in the sense of a heart-mind that is willing to see and accept the other as they *are*. It is not easy, but it can happen. It needs a lot of compassion, and also the willingness for each of us to fall into the lap of the other.'

'How does this edge you speak of allow us to go deeper than our habitual patterns?' I asked.

'I have always wished to be in a relationship which had a shared spiritual intention,' Chlöe answered. 'Now here I am in it, and I see that it is the biggest challenge I have ever had to face. Committing myself to this one relationship is an essential piece of work within the overall context of my life purpose. It also represents a particular challenge for our time.'

I asked her if she could explain what she meant.

'Well, I certainly share what you have already written on commitment,' Chlöe said. 'The woman in me who wishes to follow her own destiny, whatever that involves, the Aphrodite in me – the creative, transforming, lover aspect – used to be scared stiff at the idea of committing myself to one person. In the past, my relationships have been either with cavalier men, with whom there would be no question of commitment, or, in the case of my first marriage, with a more traditional person who provided an escape clause for my leaving because I could claim with justification that my nature could never fit into a traditional model.

'But now, with you, I am presented with someone who is a combination of the two. Your nature has something of the cavalier and yet, at the same time, there is a stability in you that welcomes the opportunity for commitment to a relationship. Now this is a mirror of my own condition, so naturally it draws me. I too am ready for an inner commitment, and this is where we meet.

'The inner commitment is to the process of our relationship as it unfolds, rather than to a particular form of it; and deeper still, it is a commitment to a shared spiritual practice and intention, whatever form that may take. The wish for a single-minded spiritual practice that one shares with one's partner inevitably affects how one experiences sexuality, the question of monogamy, and so on. The more one commits oneself internally to a spiritual practice and view of life, the more simple it is to be living in outer structures, such as marriage, that are stable and contained.'

'What is this inner practice one is committing oneself to?' I asked.

'For me,' she replied, 'it is above all about listening. Listen-

ing to an interior call which has been present throughout my
entire life and which bears no relation to my gender, cultural
upbringing, or to what I have described as my outward,
personal destiny. It bears no relation to any goddess, or to
the gods, whoever they may be. It is a listening in to
something that is beyond image; to a silent reality out of
which this life has arisen, and will return. So the listening is
to that silent reality which, like ceaseless prayer, can shape
my outer reality, which includes the reality of psychic images.'

'How does this affect your commitment to an outer relationship?' I asked.

'There is nothing more powerful, in my experience,' said
Chlöe, 'than the meeting of two beings who are joined in this
interior practice. That is why the relationship exercise we do
of listening to each other is so valuable, because it reminds us
of a level of listening that we easily forget in our day-to-day
contact. That practice can and does ripple out, though, into
the various areas of our life. Something that used to obscure
that open-minded listening was, strangely, perhaps, my
personal love for you. I am aware of looking at you with
different sets of eyes; those of the lover, the mother, the
comrade, and others; it was the motherly kind of love which
sometimes obscured what was there; the caring, nurturing love
that wanted you to be all right, satisfied and happy. Sometimes
that love did not allow me to see how you were getting in the
way of yourself, and my attempts to support you, in that case,
only tended to entrench you more deeply into your difficulty.

'The companion, comrade level, though, which is now my
most common experience of you, loves you in a different
way, a less conditioned, more spacious way with a quality of
acceptance which knows no bounds. Sheer joy in you, for no
reason. It is actually approaching a more androgynous love;
beyond gender, but not asexual – in fact, in a strange way it is
even more sexual, perhaps because the sexuality arises out of
a less conditional, broader way of seeing the other. This
other, you, fully embodies the physical lover and, at the
same time, represents that which is beyond physical love, in
a realm beyond form altogether. Not beyond it so much as

independent of it. Traditionally, as I have said earlier, men and women have had to take one of these directions or the other – the householder or the monk or the nun – not both at the same time. What we are being called to do in our time is to embrace both directions at once, which is not easy.'

'Something we have not spoken about is the impact on our relationship of our children,' I said. 'We both have a child from a previous marriage who lives with the other parent and stays with us regularly. How would you articulate this impact?'

Chlöe responded immediately. 'The presence of our children actually strengthens what commitment we have to an inner practice, though in a roundabout way,' she said. 'They show us all the time those elements and features in our respective psyches that obscure the silence we have spoken of. For me, too, my daughter has brought me up against the co-existence, not always easy, of the mother, the lover and the recluse in me. It was not long ago that I used to feel pulled in different directions.'

'It has been the same for me as a father,' I added. 'How can we bring together these three in one place?'

For a long moment, Chlöe remained quiet. When she finally spoke, she did so with a quiet authority I have come to recognise and value.

'It's only recently that I have started to see that the role of mother does not need to conflict with these other roles at all. As a parent, one is guardian of a human life and spirit. As I enter more into my own substance, I begin to experience how that substantiality is finely related to the essential, physical substance of being a nourisher and a provider. That silent reality is after all the ultimate provider, and the parent is a reflection of that in relation to the child. So there is a thread that connects our spiritual view with our personal relationship and with our children, even though they and we may not be fully aware of it. The whole theme of relationship,' she said, smiling, 'is a never-ending story. We shall need another book to give it the attention it deserves.'

— 13 —

Beauty

Mankind will be saved by Beauty. (*Fyodor Dostoevsky*)

Just as the soul in us, or the Person, is nourished by the truth of eternal ideas, so in the same way are we sustained by a contact with beauty. Though our inner cities are in decay and our forests are being razed to the ground; though utilitarian and materialist values dominate every corner of our culture, still Beauty remains everywhere on earth, and will not cease to act upon the hearts of those who are willing to see it.

What do we mean when we speak of Beauty? Like truth, it is a manifestation of original Being. It is an expression in form and matter of wholeness, of the completeness of something. It has a rightness to it, an impression of harmonic proportion, of nothing missing. It is not just this, though. There is also present in Beauty, a luminosity, or radiance, that somehow gives depth and substance to its harmonising and ordering influence.

While beauty is the light of being shining through form – and it can be any form – it needs the human heart to recognise and enunciate it. Its effect on a person sensitive to it is to draw out its qualities of wholeness, harmony and radiance from within the person themselves – to bring forth their own beauty. Beauty, then, is raised to a greater beauty in interaction; it can then be said to belong no more to the object seen than to the one who is seeing. It exists, rather, in the space between the two, as a condition of Beauty, or Being, in which both cohere.

All this, however, depends on our manner of looking, and on the quality of attention we give to what is before our eyes. It is the way we look that distinguishes the experience of Beauty from that of sensual or aesthetic pleasure – from the desire that leaps out of the eyes in response to some object of attraction. This was brought home to me graphically recently in the street. I suddenly noticed this very shapely woman who, as we passed each other, looked me in the eyes and smiled demurely. At the same instant the words, 'How beautiful you are!' involuntarily leaped from my mouth. That was our only exchange, but it altered my energy for the rest of the day. The following week I went to a local garage to have my car serviced. I sat down in the reception and there was the same woman at a typewriter behind the counter. She had not yet seen me, and for the first few seconds I felt embarrassed. My original experience and contact with her could not easily be continued in the public environment we were in, and I in any event had no wish to carry it further. I did not quite know what to do.

Then suddenly – all this happened without forethought, in a split second – I saw a different person from the one I had seen in the street: a young woman at work in her office who, with a certain shyness and self-consciousness, was in conversation with her colleagues over some detail or other. In the absence of my darting desire, she was there in her ordinariness, in her simplicity, and, I realised, in her beauty. I could see, in the midst of her daily personality, an innocence and a transparency which, here and there, in between sentences and gestures, shone through. My embarrassment vanished. Just then, our eyes met. This time I felt light, and open, with utterly no demand on the person before me, even though I was still aware of her physical form. Her look was correspondingly simple, without the seductive gaze of before. No word was needed, and nothing else needed to be done. The moment was complete in itself.

Sensual pleasure, then, before a shapely body, a bowl of fruit, the fine line of a face, or a well-conceived design, nourishes and awakens the desire body, which immediately sends a stream of energy to the stimulus. This is the perfectly natural and unceasing exchange that occurs between all living things, although the separateness between subject and object is still maintained. Beauty, however, while it, too, is felt in the body and with the senses, is also an intuitive perception of consciousness: it involves a resonance with the inherent nature and truth of a thing or a moment. There is no

separateness in a condition of Beauty, so no element needs –
even though it may do so – to travel anywhere, either in
word or in deed, unlike the leap of desire. To see Beauty is to
see the life that is alive in a person or a thing; it is to rejoin
ourselves to our family of fellow creatures; not just to
humans, but to animals and trees; to all creatures and living
things.

It is Beauty that enables us to see beyond the conventions
of fashion and style to the inner proportion and radiance of
the essential form. Such looking as this can uncover Beauty
in the most unlikely of places; in underground trains, in a
cancer ward, in the shanty towns of Bombay or Calcutta; in
the old, the fat, even the apparently ugly, whose intrinsic
beauty can sometimes shine with less obstruction than in
sleeker, though harder bodies. It can be the same with
someone near death. An old woman I once knew had
someone call me to her bedside when she was on the edge of
death. She could not speak, and I do not even know that she
could see me. She just held out her hand for me to hold. Her
body had wasted away with cancer. On the one hand she
resembled a cadaver, and yet on the other, she was more
alive than I was with a light that filled her with beauty and
lifted me into a state that was far more open and serene than
that in which I had entered the room. It was as if her
emaciated body had allowed the surfacing of a spirit that
better health and absorption in daily life had obscured.

As well as the human form, the traditional avenues of
Beauty have always been nature and art. In the arts, a work
of beauty is an alchemy of technique, expertise, and the
quality of the artist's vision and intention. It is as if a
particular state of being can somehow be mathematically
transcribed into stone, or colour, or music. If the original
impetus for making something stems from the profit motive,
an exclusive concern for functionalism; the wish to entice, or
charm; or the wish to execute a skill as cleverly as possible,
then it will of necessity sound a very different note to the
work undertaken as a labour of love, or reverence, or as
an expression of a vision that touches the deeper chords
and aspirations of a whole culture. Every shade of human

consciousness, from the most opaque to the most translucent, has its counterpart in sound and shape and colour, and the genius of art is to evoke qualities of being that live in the hearts of all but are only too rarely remembered and known.

Such genius as this is rarely known today, for art, like everything else in our culture, has largely succumbed to the secular values of the age, and to the inherent anxiety of a culture which has outgrown its old visions and has yet to find new ones. It does not serve to romanticise or pine for a time long past of soaring cathedrals and artist-monks who poured their devotion on to canvas and into stone; for as Cecil Collins has written:

> even the most devoted artists and followers of a religion find it more and more difficult to paint the standard subjects of formal religion. It is because symbols get used up and have to be returned to the unconscious to be refreshed.[17]

Neither does it serve any better than nostalgia to sever art from tradition altogether. This has been the overriding impetus of practically every school of art in the twentieth century. In her book, *Has Modernism Failed?*, Suzi Gablik remarks that

> neither science nor art in our era has been content with what has been believed before, associating traditional beliefs with backwardness and lack of momentum. But to sustain itself a society must also have values that resist change. Now, after so many metamorphoses and revolutions of every kind, we no longer know which rules we should follow, much less why, and we have destroyed the conviction that there are any limits to art at all.[18]

Even if art has been a mirror for 'the general neurosis of our time' (Jung), there are and will always be individuals whose work is the expression of a larger reality. Even so, it is to the museums and the cathedrals – to the heritage of our past – that we still must turn in order to be nourished by the beauty of art. Most museums are in fact soulless places, but an exception is the one that houses Fra. Angelico's paintings. He painted his frescoes on the walls of the cells of his fellow brothers, and they remain intact in the Museo San Marco, in Florence, the same monastery where the artist worked and prayed 600 years ago.

As I came up the monastery stairs, *The Annunciation* shone down on me from the outer wall of the cell opposite the open doorway. Another day it may have been different; that day it gathered my attention like a magnet. A few moments later I moved into the first cell and there was *The Sermon on the Mount*. As I gazed on the enraptured faces of the disciples, I distinctly sensed that the fresco was 'acting' on me. I felt myself being drawn into a state of deep silence that reflected the faces before me. It was an age that I stood there, filled with the light and grace that shone from the scene before me.

An image does not have to be the work of a master, however, or even to be an original, to draw us into an awareness of beauty. There is in my study a large picture of Jalalludin Rumi, the twelfth-century founder of the Mevlevi (Whirling) Dervishes. He is in traditional pose: kneeling, swathed in his shroud and holding a rosary, eyes open though inward. It is not that the picture was executed with any great vision or authority. The painter is anonymous; he is a copier rather than a painter: a copier of a stylised picture of Rumi that has come down through the ages. Yet the essence of a Rumi shines through: the softness of the whole composition, barely more than a sketch; the firm gaze of the eyes, wrapt in contemplation; the serenity of the face, gently inclined: all combine to evoke a mood of stillness and gathered attention. As I let the image in, it takes me into its silence. In this sense, the Rumi picture is an icon; a form designed to assist in the passage beyond form.

We do not need to be artists or visionaries or saints in order to know the nature of beauty; neither do we need to be in a museum, with our lover, or in the midst of some spectacular display of nature. Wherever we are, whatever we are doing, we can be willing to let the scales fall from our eyes and see what is there. Beauty is the quality of a moment that is complete in itself. It needs no judgement or analysis or wilful end of any kind. As we recognise it, so we are taken up into it, and our self-consciousness and sense of separateness can fall away. It is a moment in which nothing is lacking and nothing is in excess. Such a moment is not one of unconscious idyll, or infant paradise; on the contrary, beauty requires an unusual degree of consciousness to enable its manifestation. It is not, though, the consciousness of the self-reflecting, separate ego; it is the presence of the Person in us, which fosters a condition of intimacy with each other and with all things.

Kathleen Raine

— 14 —

Kathleen Raine

I wanted to continue these reflections on Beauty in the company of Kathleen Raine because she is the person I know who has done most in her long life to uphold the cause of truth and beauty in the arts. She is the co-founder and editor of *Temenos*, a review dedicated to the arts as a vehicle for the sacred; she is a poet of the first rate, and an authority on William Blake and W. B. Yeats. If there was anyone able to speak of beauty in terms of a spiritual practice and view of life, it was Kathleen Raine. At her home in Chelsea, I asked her what meaning beauty held for her.

She replied that it was impossible to speak on the subject unless one accepted the realm to which beauty belonged, the realm of the soul. Beauty simply could not be spoken of from the point of view of materialist philosophy, because in the world of 'matter', one could only speak in quantitative terms.

'We live,' she continued, 'in what Guénon has called a "reign of quantity". You can describe appearances in their manifestation in time and space but you cannot attribute qualities to them if you are operating from the time-space dimension alone. If you use a term like beauty – or any term of value – you are immediately entering the realm of consciousness and of soul. According to the Platonic tradition, which is after all our European spiritual foundation, Beauty is the supreme value, because it is the mark and signature in outward expression of truth. The good and the true can only be apprehended through the beautiful which is the form taken by these. Then we can speak of Beauty in forms because, according to the Platonic philosophy, the outer world is not separate from the spiritual world but an expression of it.'

'How,' I asked, 'are we to discern the mark and presence of Beauty?'

'It is innate, Roger, because we are ourselves spiritual beings. Beauty is an experience. Here we touch upon the ancient idea of man as a microcosm. Christianity is a very dualistic religion. It separated spirit from its embodiment almost from the beginning and this has produced a rift between the worlds of matter and of meaning and spirit. One of our tasks is surely to heal that rift, by understanding the outer world as a mirror of the inner.'

'So it is the quality of Beauty within us,' I suggested, 'that can apprehend Beauty external to us.'

Kathleen Raine paused. 'You are right, of course; that is a way of putting it that depends on the idea that they are separate. From the Hindu *advaita* (non-dual) point of view, they are not separate in the first place.'

I did not quite follow her in this. There may be no separation ultimately, but as Needleman had said, we must beware of the easy synthesis. 'Who we ordinarily take ourselves to be, though,' I suggested, 'our ordinary identity, *is* separate from that quality of being and seeing in us that is able to perceive Beauty.'

'We were all brought up in a materialist ideology,' said Kathleen Raine, 'and we are all tainted by it in some degree. The first thing that's necessary is to put this idea from us. This is hardly new. My own teacher, William Blake, radically challenged the materialism of the eighteenth century. Blake said

Nature has no outline, but Imagination has. Nature has no tune, but Imagination has. Nature has no supernatural and dissolves, Imagination is Eternity.

'He saw Nature as the mirror, a transient mirror, a flow of forms which is not an unreality but an appearance. Many biologists would say now that what we see as if out there is an appearance in the brain. There is no duality. Whatever matter is, it is not what we see. What we see is an image in our own consciousness. Duality makes the spiritual order unreal and abstract, and it withdraws from Nature and appearances the right to be called beautiful, or to have anything but a quantitative existence.'

'Are there any examples of Beauty to which you would point in our time?' I asked.

'In art, the modernist school has not set out to depict Beauty,' she replied, 'nor do they even have the word in their vocabulary. There is a whole stream of so-called art which is a direct expression of materialist ideology which itself has no place for Beauty. But if you go to Cecil Collins's exhibition at the Tate,' she continued, 'there is Beauty unveiled. No one can deny that Collins's work is a manifestation of Beauty itself. We recognise it, we know those beautiful faces and scenes of the soul's country. In general, the impact of Beauty, to any sensitive person, is immediate. Then, there is always Nature. And there is also always one another, and the extraordinary mystery of love. Love is epiphanic. To fall in love is to see another human being in their beauty. That in itself is a divine epiphany.'

'And the person in whom one sees Beauty,' I remarked, 'may not conform to a stereotyped idea of beauty at all. So the standard conventions of beauty are not what we are talking about, are they?'

'Absolutely not. In fact the glossy magazine, by its exclusive concern with the physical, precludes beauty – however "attractive" or desirable the men and women in them may appear to be. The beauty in glossy photographs is purely external. Yet one can see the Beauty we are speaking of in ugly faces. Socrates said, didn't he, "make me beautiful within"? What you see when you see another's Beauty is their soul.'

What Kathleen was saying reminded me of Frederick Franck's drawings. Author of *Zen in the Art of Seeing*, Franck seems able to capture in his drawings the intrinsic Beauty of elderly, and often large, women. I mentioned this in passing.

'Yes, and Rembrandt was the same,' Kathleen added. 'Rembrandt painted the old because that is when the physical frame begins to melt away and you see the soul. You can have beauty in young faces, of course, but Beauty is always immeasurable. What, then, do a women's measurements have to do with her Beauty?'

'Though in antiquity,' I pointed out, 'proportion was one of the guiding principles of Beauty.'

Kathleen Raine picked up the point quickly. 'As indeed in certain contexts it still is,' she said. 'Because the world is structured on number, generating forms. So, in a sense, the whole world is a formal structure, from simple geometric forms to the most complex. In that sense, there is a Beauty in Nature itself. But when these sacred proportions are reduced to purely quantitative mathematics, the Beauty of natural forms is obscured. The unstructured kind of modern art like Jackson Pollock's has lost touch with the intrinsic harmony of form altogether, so he was depicting neither form nor Beauty. I cannot imagine what such painters are trying to say, unless they are trying to draw everything out of themselves to see what is there. But unless you implicitly accept soul and spirit, and the unity of outer and inner, there will be this schizophrenia in art. Collins has returned the sacred to art in England. Music has been the same. Musicians have been sacrificing and losing form. Soul is form, and embodiment is the soul's "signature" or "correspondence". As Spenser wrote, "For soul is form and doth the body make".'

I then turned to the question of standing before an artifact which was not necessarily a great work of art, and yet which nevertheless evoked a state of presence and silence – as in the case of my own picture of Rumi. Could that picture therefore be seen as an expression of Beauty, I asked, even if it were a mediocre work of art?

'A bad playing of a Bach fugue may be very far from perfection,' she said, 'but to hear one's child play a simple piece can stir something. The person who responds to the bad religious painting is responding to the archetype, not the depiction. The village idols in India are crude bits of clay dressed up in rags, but to the villagers they communicate the archetype of the god. I think the insincerity of much religious art actually speaks louder than the archetype, but even then, the most sentimental pictures can have meaning for a child, and for anyone for whom the archetype of the picture is a reality. There can be a snobbism in art which makes a religion of the execution itself. When the goal becomes the sophistication and perfection of the execution, the contact with the archetype is lost. That is when the question is raised, when is an idol an icon, and when is an icon an idol? A crude idol can sometimes communicate what the best executed of paintings cannot.'

'That depends,' I said, 'on how we ourselves see. What is this quality of seeing which can enable us to see another in their beauty, or that can encourage the archetype to leap out of a crude figure of clay?'

'To discard the obstacles in the way is the first task,' she answered. 'We won't see anything if we are in a bad mood, or if we are seeing from the vantage point of an opaque ideology. "Every pebble on the ground was like a precious jewel," said Traherne. It is all there, you see. You don't need to see a peacock to think a bird beautiful; a sparrow will do just as well. It's a fallacy to think you have to go to the Lake District to see natural beauty. A piece of chickweed in the sidewalk has beauty too, if you can see it. Sometimes this seeing is given as a grace.'

'But surely one can make an invitation to it?'

'Oh yes, and gradually over time it can become your normal way of seeing the world, as a result of a certain orientation. Moments of grace can inspire faith in this kind of vision. Falling in love is one such grace. One moment this person looks just like anyone else, and the next, you see them revealed in their uniqueness, in their real nature. Love is not blind, you know, it is a higher vision of reality.' She spoke boldly, with a determined smile; well aware of the un-psychological nature of her view. 'It can be the same with nature. I am sure I echo the experience of many when I say I have seen a plant suddenly transform into a living being before my eyes; into an awe-inspiring beauty of luminous light. The idea of the plant being an object in an external world was instantaneously removed by this revelation. It must have been the same with Traherne. What was dead becomes living. So many people are forced by the unspoken assumptions of the media culture into seeing a dead universe.

If one can only remove this illusion one can see the world and oneself to be alive . . .'

' . . . and therefore beautiful,' I added.

'And therefore beautiful, yes. The opposite of Beauty, you know, is the commonplace, the dead – not the ugly. The ugly is a form of Beauty, a form of meaning. The dragons, the gargoyles, are as much a part of the world of the soul as angelic forms.'

'Dragons are certainly very alive,' I added. 'The mechanistic, then, is the opposite to the beautiful?'

Kathleen Raine was thoughtful for a moment. 'In a sense,' she replied, 'though, really, there is no opposite to being. Another block,' she went on, 'to the vision we have been speaking of, is sentimentality. Sentimentality arises when we do not see nature as living, and we pretend that it is beautiful. Or thinking that one thing in nature is better or worse than another; what a beautiful cat, but what a horrible beetle.'

'So Beauty,' I said, 'actually goes beyond the dilemma of the opposites, beyond our idea of like and dislike?'

Kathleen Raine replied firmly. 'Yes,' she said, 'because the dilemma of the opposites is an attribute of the mechanistic world. Being as such, the world of the soul, has no opposite. Preference is ours; it is not inherent in the world as it is in itself.' She then went on to make another point. 'In India, practically everyone is beautiful, old and young, poor and ragged, because in that country, people still live as a whole in the world of soul. It's not just the beauty of their bone structure, or anything like that, that makes them beautiful; it is a culture imbued with being. In the cities, that has already changed, the secular has invaded just like anywhere else. In Bombay, for example, you can see the same ethnic face, but without beauty.'

'In speaking of a culture that emanates Beauty, you are speaking of a coherent culture, aren't you?' I asked. 'One that has an inherent unity. We live in a fragmented culture, and traditionally, Beauty has always implied integrity, unity.'

For a moment, Kathleen Raine was silent, as if she were remembering a time when that integrity still reigned. Then

she turned to me. 'Yes,' she said quietly, 'form gives co-
herence, unity. That's what form is. Jung really did give our
culture a key to a door which is in everyone, and that is our
dreams. Whatever one dreams is not neutral or dead. It is
either terrifying or beautiful, and it speaks for itself. Dreams
can shake us out of our "deadly sleep", as Blake said. The
archetypes are in us, after all. We know innately what a tree
means, and the sun, and the moon, and so on, and in our
dreams, if we do not let the interpreting rational mind get in
the way, we are left in no doubt.

'If Beauty relates to the soul's country, that country is a
non-dual reality. Henri Corbin invented the term "imaginal
world", which is an inter-world between the outer world and
the spiritual world, which has abstract ideas but no form.
This imaginal world is the region of Beauty because it
embodies; soul cannot ever be without form. This is the
world of archetypes. Of course you can encounter the
archetype in the physical world no less than in a dream. The
archetype only truly speaks through the natural world when
the natural world is experienced within the living unit of
inner and outer. Then you cannot properly say that the sun
"represents" light or illumination. Blake said, when asked,
"Do you not perceive a round disc, somewhat like a guinea?"
"Oh no, I perceive a multitude of heavenly hosts singing
holy, holy, holy." He didn't say the sun made him think of
the heavenly host, the sun *is* that. This is the true encounter
with the archetype in the outer, natural world.'

This is the true encounter with Beauty. Soon after she had
finished speaking, I got up to go. In my mind as I left were
four brief lines she included in her *Collected Poems 1935–1980*:

I've read all the books but one
Only remains sacred: this
Volume of wonders, open
Always before my eyes.[19]

— 15 —

Suffering

The pain of life is the price paid
For the quickening of the heart.

(Hazrat Inayat Khan)

What follows is not a eulogy of suffering, in the vein of the old British school which believed it was good for you. I would certainly not wish suffering on anybody, including myself. It is, however, though we may long to rid the earth of it, an integral part of existence; an expression of the limitation that constricts all forms of life, not least to a certain span. Suffering, whether we wish it or not, is part of what is.

So, too, are pain and pleasure, though they are a different matter. They usually describe events local to a particular aspect or dimension of our being. My foot hurts; it is a pleasure to be massaged; I was pained by what you said; it was a pleasure to see him again. Suffering, and also joy, refer to experiences that pervade the whole of who we know ourselves to be, body, mind and soul. This is why we defend ourselves, for the most part unconsciously, from their impact: both joy and suffering in their different ways can dissolve our sense of control and the borders of the separate ego. This is a double-edged moment: it may lead to disintegration on the one hand, or to a more complete integration on the other. Who can say, in the case of any one individual, which way it will go?

Neither can we console ourselves with the thought that each individual receives the measure of suffering they can bear. It is not so simple. We have only to look at any day's newspaper, or to listen to the talk in a local store, to hear of people who have been crushed by their suffering through no obvious fault of their own.

Suffering, whether we wish it or not, is the case; and the truth is, we do not understand it. The greatest part of it seems to serve no purpose whatsoever other than the wearing down of the human spirit. The question is whether this always needs to be so. There were people in the German concentration camps who died in joy, praying for the forgiveness of their murderers. After ten days without food, most people would say they were starving. Yet Gandhi did not consider himself to be starving during his hunger strikes. Our suffering, then, is determined by the mental and spiritual context within which we are able to experience it. If suffering is experienced within a large enough life perspective, it may not be felt as suffering at all – which does not mean that it will not be painful.

We also know that suffering can be the agent that provides the very pressure and intensity needed to propel a person into a broader and deeper view of themselves and of life. I have met people with cancer who are radiant. The immediacy and poignancy of realising the imminence of their death has brought them alive in a way they never knew. In some way their suffering has enabled them to surrender, to let go of their habitual hold on life and the identity they had within it. For them, suffering was transformed into joy and they became larger and more substantial human beings because of it.

Dominique Lapierre, the writer of *The City of Joy*, an extraordinary book on life in the slums of Calcutta, discovered the same thing there:

> the miracle of these concentration camps was that the accumulation of disastrous elements was counterbalanced by other factors that allowed their inhabitants not merely to remain fully human but even to transcend their condition and become models of humanity. In these slums people actually put love and mutual support into practice. They know how to give respect to a stranger, how to show charity towards beggars, cripples, lepers, even the insane. Here the weak were helped, not trampled upon.[20]

This, however, can be the point where we may be on the verge of romanticising human indignity. For every person whose suffering brought them more alive, there were dozens at the Cancer Help Centre, where I worked as a therapist for a time, whose life became progressively cramped into a smaller and smaller part of their being. For every person mentioned in *The City of Joy*, there are millions in alleyways, in deserts, in prison camps, all over the world, who are being crushed by the hopelessness of their predicament. It would be an error, then, and a dangerous one, to assume that because suffering has been seen to transform a personality, it can do so anywhere, and in anyone's case. The possible is always determined by the constraints of the actual mental and physical condition of the particular individual, for which there are few who can act as judge.

I have never personally experienced real suffering deriving from a physical source – hunger, illness, injury, or poverty. On the relatively few occasions when I have been witness to it – working on a homeless project in London; in my work at the Cancer Centre in Bristol; in India, and other Third World countries – it has opened my heart to others and to some awareness, though transitory, of my own inevitable decay and death. It has made me sensitive to our inter-being: to the fact that the joy or suffering of another is my own, and that we all share the essential aspects of the human predicament. To know our own or another's suffering we need to be porous, open to the great currents of deep feeling that course through the fabric of human experience, so often far beneath the surface of our daily awareness.

Often, however, we are not open in this way. On the contrary, the suffering we are witness to can close us down through the fear of being blown away. This is what happened to me in Benares. If you want to reach the banks of the Ganges in that city, you have to walk down a whole street full of beggars, all of whom are maimed or disfigured in every imaginable way. Having arrived at the river's edge, I was assailed by a dozen or more youths and men, all desperate for my custom on one or other of the boats.

After ten minutes at the oars my chosen boatman, no more than 16, began to sweat and gasp for breath. A few minutes more and he could hardly row. He struggled to turn the boat round, saying he had to go back to get his fix. He was a heroin addict, and, he told me, so was nearly every other boy along the shore. My limit was reached when he told me that they bought their supplies from the doctors, who would pilfer the city hospitals' supplies. At that moment the whole city felt to me like hell on earth. I retreated for the rest of the afternoon to my room. The condition I was in was simply not large enough to embrace the impressions I was receiving, and I lost my orientation in a mixture of outrage, sadness and despair.

What I might have done, but didn't, is to see the strange humour in the situation of me the passenger rowing the boatman back to the shore. Sometimes, spontaneous and genuine humour can be the only lever there is on to another broader perspective – especially in the blackest of moments. In *How Can I Help?* by Ram Dass, there is the extraordinary story that Wavy Gravy, the clown, tells of his visit to a children's hospital.

There was this one little black kid. He was horribly burned. He looked like burnt toast. Pieces of his face weren't there. Pieces of his ears were missing. Where was his mouth? You could hardly tell who he was. There was no way of pinning a person to this face, what little there was of it. It was terrible. Just mind-boggling. My jaw dropped. He was unbelievably painful to behold.

All of a sudden, this other little kid comes whizzing by, skating along with his IV pole. He stops, and looks into the crib at this other kid, and comes out with, 'Hey, YOU UGLY!' Just like that. And the burnt kid made this gurgling laugh kind of noise and his face moved around.

'YOU UGLY!' Right. He ugly. And if he's gotta deal with people hanging around with saliva coming out of their mouths, it's gonna be extra horrible. But if somebody just meets him in the eye and say, 'Hey, what's happening? Wanna hear a riddle...?'[21]

In Benares, however, it all felt overwhelmingly serious. My emotions plunged me into a dramatisation of the suffering which was probably unknown either to the beggars or to the addict. Being intense by its very nature, suffering naturally attracts our instinct for dramatisation, which is always wanting *something*, even anything, to happen, so that we can have the sensation that we are happening ourselves. Elaborating on the drama of suffering, giving free rein to the emotions that are generated and using it as a principle subject of conversation, is a royal way of actually avoiding the full impact of the suffering itself. Instead of passing through it, or letting it pass through and over us, we become our suffering. We then have something to speak about. This is also why we can be reluctant to let it go. After all, without our troubles, who are we?

If we can avoid the actuality of suffering by over-identifying with it, we can also avoid it by retreating to the wisdom of the inner eye, which can see from its cool and silent, all-encompassing vision, that everything is happening just as is meant. Wise as it is, if we cling to this position for safety we forego our connectedness with the rest of humanity and with our own human heart. Can we allow the pain and sorrow of our human frailty while *at the same time* being aware of a dimension in which all is well and will ever continue to be so? This is one of the questions with which suffering confronts us.

In contemporary culture we have created a different arena for suffering than the poverty and disease of developing countries. Everyone in our culture is in some degree at the mercy of a suffering that stems from a mental/emotional, and also a spiritual source. It is not for that any the less painful or insidious in its effects than physical suffering. Mother Teresa once said that our culture was more in need of help than the destitute she served in Calcutta.

Either loneliness or relationship difficulties usurp a portion of our attention and time that would be inconceivable in a culture of extended families and close-knit communities. Again, our tendency is to avoid the suffering of the situation by either turning it into a colourful drama or to rise above it altogether. In my first marriage I took the latter course. When it finally ended, we were both deeply relieved. We both saw ourselves constrained by an incompatibility we were unable to resolve. It was damaging to us both, and also to our child, and we knew that for everyone's health we had to withdraw.

Our divorce, then, generated simultaneous and contradictory feelings in me. On the one hand, I felt liberated and returned to myself. On the other, I was keenly aware that my own relief was at the expense of my son's pain and acute sense of loss. Yet if my wife and I had attempted to stay together for his sake, something essential in us would have been denied and he would still not have got what he really wanted, a context of family love between his parents. The story is familiar to many. I simply had to accept the contradiction and the impossibility of the situation. Sometimes I have been trapped by the consequent guilt and grief; more often I have clung to the intuition that all shall be well, for my son as well as for us. At times, I have stood in both places at once, and my grief has become one aspect of a larger pattern of life in the process of an inevitable unfolding.

My divorce softened me, and humbled me, too. It brought me down to earth, and made it glaringly obvious how my life was not working. It brought home to me my pride, and my cowardice. It may have saved others a great deal of pain if I had been able to see these things in myself without having to pass with them through this particular fire. That, however, was not to be, and I hold no blame or recriminations against myself. My pride and my cowardice are still present, though somewhat more integrated now into my conscious picture of my personality. In some measure, at least, the suffering incurred in my marriage did its work: it provided a chastening appraisal of my actual, as distinct to my potential, condition; frequently, I have a propensity to confuse the two.

Our culture suffers too, through the deep lack and the struggle for meaning. Intensified by the dizzying pace of cultural change, our search for identity and stability often centres around the attempt to find meaningful work. Achievement and success in the world may certainly fulfil our need for a social identity, as well as confirming the value of our creative energy. They are the fruits of the urge in us to become, and they can certainly give meaning of a kind. They do not and cannot, however, fulfil a deeper need, which is the inherent wish to be – not this, or that, but simply to be, alive in the fullness of existence.

The suffering associated with the question of meaning stems ultimately from this deeper layer. We cannot always ignore the suspicion that none of our activities and achievements, or our ideas of who we are – including any philosophy or religion we may hold to – actually contains anything of substance that we can point to as being our essential identity. I cannot, if I look, find myself anywhere in them. The great fear that accompanies this realisation is that I do not exist at all. I am empty, without substance, no-thing. This nothing, not acknowledged or entered into, can wear away for a lifetime at the substance we may imagine ourselves to be. It can enter into our very body as tensions and places of dullness that seem to have no cause. It may not allow us to rest in anything or anyone, or fully to place our feet on the earth at all, for fear that we may be caught and our insubstantiality revealed.

I have known something of this suffering. It is the kind that can creep unrecognised into any and every moment of the day, in the guise of not being quite content with what I have, and wanting what I do not have. Nothing is quite right, so to speak. In constantly busying ourselves with moving the furniture around, or even bringing in different furniture altogether, we avoid the inherent emptiness and space of the room.

Finally, there is the suffering that accompanies the longing for something not of this world. So often, it is expressed in terms of a lover to the Beloved. The following verse is by 'Ayn al-Qozat Hamadani, a Sufi who was executed in Baghdad in 1131 on a charge of heresy:

Long as I live I'll eat and drink
the sorrow of loving you
nor will I surrender it, this sorrow,
to anyone when I am dead.
Tomorrow
when Resurrection comes
I'll walk forth with this raging thirst
still in my head [22]

Yet none of this suffering, however existential or spiritual its roots may be, will take us very far unless we actually come to the point of deciding to engage with it and to take it on, consciously. This is what distinguished Gandhi from the starving. Renunciation, though – which is conscious suffering – is not necessarily dependent on an external act: it is essentially an inner decision to stand firm against the majority in ourselves – the larger part of us, our tendencies, preferences and comfortable habits – which normally and automatically lead us down the path of least resistance. I easily follow my fear, my anger, my righteousness, without question; I also continue to console myself with the bittersweet pain of the longing rather than go where the longing is wanting to take me. I will flirt with the occasional intimation of my mortality and impermanence; feeling the heat of it but rarely present enough to go any closer. The willingness to forego my consolations and to suffer the truth of my whole condition without preferring one aspect of it over the other: its substance and its emptiness; its sensuality and its wish for the eternal; my distaste for this and my attraction to that; my arrogance and my humility: this, I know, is the fire that can forge someone new. Can I dare, though, to enter it rather than cover my tracks with more words? Do I want the truth enough to be able to make that kind of effort? The answer is no; and occasionally, yes. There is a truth I do not find easy to bear. No blame.

— 16 —

Work

... All knowledge is vain save when there is work,
And all work is empty save when there is love;
And when you work with love, you bind yourself to
yourself, and to one another, and to God.
And what is it to work with love?

It is to weave the cloth with threads drawn from
your heart, even as if your beloved were to wear that
cloth.
It is to build a house with affection, even as if
your beloved were to dwell in that house.
It is to sow seeds with tenderness and reap the
harvest with joy, even as if your beloved were to
eat the fruit...
Work is love made visible.

(Kahlil Gibran, *The Prophet*)[23]

Why is the whole question of work so often a problem?
Because so often we are. Because the ancient blessing–curse
is upon our heads. This brings fear, self-protection and the
struggle for survival, much of which turns on the nature of
our activity, and the rewards it is to bring us. This is only the
beginning: there is then the matter of our personal identity
and the search for self-confirmation through meaningful
activity; not to mention the fact that work is the arena in
which we most commonly engage with others and the
community at large, a challenge of a lifetime in itself. Finally,
there are some who endeavour to make their work an
expression of their deepest commitment to God, with results
varying from holy wars and mass baptisms on the one hand,
to, on the other, anonymous saints who give their lives to
serving the poor of the world's ghettos and slums. With so

many issues converging on to the activity we call work, it is hardly surprising that most of us find it a headache at one time or another.

We know that it was not always so, and is still not the case in the few traditional cultures that survive. There, as in the not-so-distant past of our own culture, one is born into an activity that one accepts without question. Sometimes there are good years and sometimes there are bad ones. There is a natural rhythm of storing up reserves in times of plenty for times of scarcity. Sometimes there is not enough, and some people may die. Death, too, is an inevitable part of the cycle. Personal meaning comes from fulfilling the social duties of family and one's inherited activity, which of necessity is beneficial to the community as a whole. One's work is not so much one's personal work, something one has created out of one's own imagination, as a role designated by the needs of the community. Then there are religious festivals and seasonal offerings to the gods that bind one's work to the larger cosmic round. In traditional communities, the notion of work itself is a foreign one. There is rather the rhythmic process of life in which all the various activities, relationships and functions, form an intricate and integral whole.

We have come a very long way since then and are unlikely ever to return; though it is arguable whether the direction we have travelled is necessarily forwards. Our culture still holds quite firmly to the Darwinian belief in an unremitting progress from the lower stages of consciousness to successively higher ones. Certainly the world has changed in the span of a few years almost beyond recognition. Imagine what South Korea was like just twenty years ago, or Saudi Arabia forty years ago. Forty years ago, the South of France was still principally a land of shepherds and fishermen, who lived and died in the vicinity of their birthplace. Now we live in a culture which, increasingly liberated from the necessity of being tied to just one place with one occupation, is constantly on the move.

It may not seem surprising that we regard our ancestors from the vantage point of a certain superiority, and ourselves as having advanced almost to being a different race altogether. The evolutionary spiral exists without question. The false assumption that it draws along in its slipstream is that more equals qualitatively better. Huston Smith, in his book, *Forgotten Truth*, says:

> Not that the higher appears after the lower, but that it is produced by the lower – this is what tradition denies. In doing so it counters the dominant mood of our time. Order from revolution (Marx), ego from id (Freud), life from the primal ooze (Darwin); everywhere the reflexive impulse is to derive the more from the less. Tradition proceeds otherwise.[24]

Then, a few pages later:

> The evolutionary cycle is not denied: amoebas did come first; life does advance. It is the claim that everything about man can be accounted for by a process, natural selection, that works mechanically on chance variations – this is the false claim.[25]

Since the Renaissance, man has held ever more firmly to the belief in his inherent capacity for self-creation and self-transformation. In the nineteenth century, Nietzsche insisted that evolution pointed beyond physical adaptation (Darwin) towards ever greater creative excellence, towards the superman who was a pioneer of self-realisation. More than anywhere else, the philosophy of self-creation has expressed itself in the arena of work in the world. Whereas the Renaissance ideal still had its roots in the transcendental – its concern was an inner, rather than an outer work – our present entrepreneurial society draws its inspiration from the Protestant work ethic and the Victorian image of the self-made man. An extraordinary idea which is inherent in all spiritual practice has become utterly humanised, secularised, and identified with our capacity for growth and activity.

Action is the order of the day. Our culture is addicted to intensity and compulsive activity, and we validate our addiction by collectively agreeing that action is what changes things, gets them moving, and improves our inner and outer conditions. And, of course, it does, as we have already seen. The investment we have made in activity, however, and the way we go about it, are at a cost of which we are barely aware. As Wendell Berry remarks; 'the pattern of industrial "development" on the farm, in the forest, as in the coal fields, is that of combustion and exhaustion – not "growth"'.[26] Many find that the exhaustion is not only of external, but of internal resources as well. Then, although our furious productivity has put us in a league of our own in terms of the realm of quantity, it is not at all obvious that the values and motivations underpinning our culture are any more founded on wisdom, compassion, justice, dignity, or truth, than those of the Greeks or the Romans.

None of this is to imply, of course, that we should do nothing to improve or change our lot. The very essence of life is movement, action, and we shall always act, for good or ill, whether we wish it or not. The point is, we cannot squeeze out of activity what it simply does not and cannot contain. It is this that causes our exhaustion. By getting in on the action and making it all happen, what we really want is to feel that we are happening, that we are going to derive lasting meaning and existence – liberation from death – through our works. But fulness, meaning, wisdom, contentment, these are not of the temporal world alone. All quantitative phenomena, including our subjective identities, eventually pass away. We suspect this; we can taste our inherent emptiness and we struggle to arrange conditions in such a way as might fill the gap. What we are seeking is simply in another octave, in another qualitative direction; not elsewhere in a different place but in the unconditioned dimension of our own existence and of life itself.

We are not necessarily, then, any the happier for the work and the activity we engage in, nor even for the rewards they may bring us. There are ways in which growth, development and self-improvement simply do not deliver the goods. Though the majority of us continues to act in the same way as ever, our culture is at a time of profound self-questioning and doubt. In the world of art, for example, the postmodern thinker disputes the claim – which held sway from the Renaissance to existentialism – that humanity makes its own history. The danger stalking the postmodern labyrinth is *nothingness.* The empty tomb. The paralysing fear is that there is nothing *after* post modernism.[27]

In today's principle artistic movement, then, the hope that the future may bring something new, or better, has gone. On the other hand, the rapidly growing interest in spirituality is strongly coloured by a fascination for the other worldly: for the occult, the psychic, the angelic and the astral realms, with a strong predilection for the receiving of messages and the seeing of lights. Mainstream materialism is producing the reactions of nihilism on the one hand and a celestial flight from matter and its attendant duties on the other.

However, while most of us are either trapped in the materialist work ethic or rebelling against it, there are increasing numbers who are seeing the very nature of work in the world as a bridge between the sacred and the secular, the qualitative and quantitative, realms. Organisations now exist, such as the Business Network, to recontextualise the idea of work in the light of a broader, spiritual view of life. Under the aegis of the United Nations, there is even a Right Livelihood Award, conferred upon someone whose work has been of special benefit to humanity. It is precisely because our work can span so many layers of needs and meaning in us that it can act as such a bridge. No other dimension of our life has the same potential to connect our survival needs with our need for personal identity and meaning, with our contribution to the community, and with our sense of participation in a larger transpersonal world of meaning. Work is a bridge when all of these levels are occurring at once. As we shift from level to level, so our perspective on the value and meaning of work will change.

As we have already seen, our habitual, linear, thinking will tend to start from the bottom and attempt to work its way up. Survival needs then become the driving force. Some day, we hope, we shall make enough money to retire early and be free to do what we really love. As many have already discovered, however, this formula does not work. If, instead, we follow the ancient view that the lower derives from the higher, this familiar formula is turned on its head: we see that our security needs will most naturally be met, almost as a matter of course, when we give our attention to what we really love now, rather than later. What we are likely to discover, though, is that we are barely conscious of what our love may be. It is often so close to us that we do not recognise it. It is, anyway, beyond the scope of reason: our energy, passion and aliveness originate from the unconditioned realm of our nature. We cannot simply expect to 'work out' our place in the world. J. G. Bennett says, in *The Way To Be Free*:

> We labour under the misapprehension that we have to think up what we have to do. The truth is that this is not our responsibility, because the pattern of things is far greater than we can imagine . . . The direct perception of our pattern belongs to conscience and the unconditioned side of our nature. The pattern is creative and created.[28]

Rather than 'deciding' on what to do, our task is more to let the 'higher' in us inform the lower: which may simply mean having the faith to follow our nose. One connection, though, between the different levels in us is the memory. Recalling a time, a moment, when we felt our spontaneous joy and aliveness, when we felt close to something authentic in us, can remind us of what it is that, below our more superficial wants and desires, truly moves us. In my case, the feeling of my own aliveness soars whenever I connect with the memory of being in a wild and remote country.

What moves us, if we follow it in faith, will trace out a way for us in the affairs of the world. Arising out of this particular love of mine is a small but viable commercial initiative for leading 'journeys' to various parts of the world. It was preceded, however, by years of daydreaming and lack of conviction in the premise that the lower evolves from the higher, and not the other way around.

When our work is an echo of our unself-conscious energy and passion, it not only allows us to survive at a level we are content with; it can also engender a relatively stable identity and a sense of personal meaning. This is the common aim and limit of most contemporary psychology: self-actualisation, a term first coined by Abraham Maslow in the early 1960s.

To bring our calling into the world is, however, already to extend beyond ourselves. It is already to join with the larger community of humanity.

> The constant perfection or practice of a right livelihood will give you a view of the whole world in a sense similar to Hemingway's story of the old man's life as a fisherman, which gives him a connection with the entire world, and a whole world of experience! What are the rewards?
>
> Right livelihood has within itself its own rewards: it deepens the person who practises it. Ageing works for you in the right livelihood. It's like a good pipe or a fine violin, the more you use it, the deeper its finish.[29]

In serving others we fulfil ourselves, but the nature of service is not as evident as it may appear. There are many in the helping professions who are disillusioned, and there are those of a religious persuasion who, force-feeding themselves on the notion of charity and putting everyone else first, may be inwardly bitter and resentful. On the other hand, someone who is doing the most menial of jobs may be of deeper service to his entire environment by the manner and the light with which he or she does what he does. It is not what we do that determines an act of service; it is the dimension in ourselves that we do it from. Whatever we do out of fear will subtly separate us from others; whatever we do from the fulness of ourselves will in some way be of service.

> I'm ninety-two years old, all right. I get up every morning at seven a.m. Each day I remind myself, 'Wake up. Get up.' I talk to my legs, 'Legs get moving. Legs,

you're an antelope.' It's a matter of mind over matter. You have to have the right spirit. And I'm out on the streets, seven thirty a.m. sharp.

I'm wearing my Honorable Sanitation Commissioner badge they gave me from City Hall. I'm alert, I'm ready, I'm out there. And I got my whistle. My job is I help get parked cars off the street so they can bring in the sanitation trucks and the Wayne Broom, the big one – thirty grand for a broom! So when they show up, I go around blowing my whistle to get people to move their cars. I have a great time.

People are asleep. They're busy with businesses. They're busy taking time off from the businesses. They're busy having a good time. They're busy not having a good time. Whatever. I don't care. I blow my whistle. I'm all over the place.

. . . Everybody loves it, everybody understands. It's the whistle that gets them. Sometimes I'm having such a laugh, I can't blow it.

. . . What can I tell you? I'm not a saint or a wise man. I'm not the Two-Thousand-Year-Old-Man, I'm only the ninety-two-year-old man. Just a senior citizen. But what do I know that everybody doesn't know? We know. I just go out there in the morning and blow my whistle. That's what I do. You do what you do. Me, I'm having a great time. Wonderful fun. And when people see how much fun I'm having, they have to laugh. What else can they do? Then I hit them with it: 'Move your car!'[30]

While self-actualisation is a process and not a point of arrival, it may still never connect to an altogether different level in us which falls outside the affairs of the world altogether – which falls below even our most passionate interest and love for this or that activity. Again, when we slip from one qualitative realm to another, all the laws seem to go in reverse.

When we begin to suspect that what we truly seek is not to be found in any particular activity at all, not even in the work of our calling, then the wisdom of 'do what you love' is reversed into 'love what you do'. Here our activities and priorities take on an altogether new light. All and every experience can then begin to take on value and meaning, at the same time as the realisation that ultimate meaning is to be found in no external experience at all. Even an instant of seeing this is the beginning of living and acting in the midst of the world, while at the same time being not of it. Work undertaken in this spirit gathers all the levels we have spoken of into one. This is the work, the work and call of a lifetime, that fuses the secular with the sacred.

No longer, in that moment, expecting from work and worldly activity what it cannot give (an enduring sense of substance and identity) there is not the same investment and anxiety about its end results. It follows that if one is no longer constrained by the necessity for a specific result, then nothing essentially can go wrong. With nothing to go wrong, there can be nothing to fear. With nothing to fear, there is a dying to the customary dynamics of the world and of the everyday self, whose inner structure is founded on the tension between hope and fear. The greater truth of the ancient idea of self-creation can only occur in the wake of this dying. The true work goes on in the darkness. What may be forged, the soul of a person, is not of the ordinary world.

Paradoxically, far from causing us to withdraw from life, this kind of dying, even for a moment, allows us to abandon ourselves fully into it without reserve. After all, what else is there to do, or to lose? We act in this case not for one good reason or another, but simply out of our unfettered love of it all, of life and of others. It is this quality of action rather than the particular action itself, which finally renders it of value or not. What it will never do is to guarantee or sustain somebody's identity because there is no sense of anybody in particular doing it.

Action of this kind gathers together the totality of who we are. Its greatest mystery is this: that the very lack of self-consciousness and concern it arises from is itself the very sense of substance and somebodyness we normally busy ourselves looking for everywhere else.

Ram Dass

— 17 —

Ram Dass

'Do you know the story of my father giving me the railroad business to run when I was hardly twenty-five?' We were eating chicken fried rice somewhere in Boston in 1986. Yes, I did have a vague memory of some such story, but the details had escaped me. Ram Dass proceeded to fill them in. That lunch lasted three hours. We had to be gently nudged by the waiter to realise they were waiting to close. Three hours of being, laughter, and sharing our lives.

Why, though, might I have known the railroad story? Or any of the others that I heard that day? The question came to me only later, and the answer was obvious. Ram Dass is perhaps the major living public representative of the Western seeker. His life has become a legend, certainly in America, and to some extent in Europe as well. In this mythic sense his outer life and its various dramas are public property. He recounts the stories almost as if they belong more to the listener than to himself, with an amused detachment culti-vated, I suspect, by years of work extricating him from the popular confusion of identity, between actor and role.

The legend began in the fiery days of the 1960s, when as Richard Alpert, a Harvard psychology professor in league with Timothy Leary, he was sacked for turning his students on to LSD. Then came India, the meeting with his guru Neem Karoli Baba, and the publication of *Be Here Now*, a real landmark of its time. Neem Karoli died in 1973, and through-out that decade Ram Dass, as Neem Karoli named him, plunged into an all-consuming study and practice of Buddhist meditations, Tibetan tantric teachings and yogic disciplines. He was responsible for bringing Muktananda to the West, and helped Chogyam Trungpa found the Naropa Institute of

Buddhist Studies in Boulder, Colorado. Other books followed, *The Only Dance There Is, Grist for the Mill*, and in 1980, *Miracle of Love*, a collection of personal stories and experiences with Neem Karoli Baba, gathered from his devotees. It was in *Miracle of Love* that I first really met Ram Dass. I read it in 1980 and found tears rolling down my cheeks without knowing why. Ever since then I have felt inexplicably and intimately connected not only with Ram Dass, but also to that mysterious Indian figure, Neem Karoli Baba.

Then, in 1984, I found myself at Badrinath, a temple 12,000 feet up in the Himalayas, sufficiently spectacular, remote and away from the likes of myself to satisfy the yearnings of both the romantic and the contemplative in me. Within an hour an American had arrived. Who should it be but the Director of the Living Dying Project, an agency Ram Dass set up in the States several years ago to offer spiritual counselling to the dying. I had wanted to make contact with the Living Dying Project for some time. I forgot about the contemplative, and in the next 24 hours we shared a room, a lot of talk, and a certain amount of common work experience, since I was then a counsellor at the Bristol Cancer Help Centre. We parted friends, with a tentative agreement to consider working together with Ram Dass on a new Living Dying Centre in Boston. The new centre never happened, but the Badrinath meeting led to the Boston lunch, which in turn led to Ram Dass's visits to Europe for the Open Gate in the late 1980s.

So what was the railroad story? Well, it was really about Ram Dass's early relationship to power – power and authority in relation to others. Being in the limelight brings its own difficulties. He has always attracted positions of power, and has usually found himself side-stepping them.

Though he has a strong following he has consistently avoided having a centre or a formal group of students. When Neem Karoli died, some of his followers looked to Ram Dass to take up the succession, as a kind of Head Boy, a proposal that Ram Dass managed to diffuse by referring to the authority of his guru. Neem Karoli had told him that rather than being a formal teacher in this life, Ram Dass should commit himself to a life of service in the more general sense.

This is what he has done. He has worked with the people that few others want to work with. Apart from the Living Dying Centres, he has catalysed work in prisons. He rightly saw the many similarities between a prison and a monastery, and realised it was an ideal context for spiritual practice, especially for those on Death Row. His most recent book is *How Can I Help?*, a rich presentation on the nature of service.

Ram Dass was until recently the Chairman of the Seva Foundation, an international relief agency, and he continues to be centrally involved in the organisation's policies and direction. I know no better person with whom to discuss the question of how work might be envisioned as service, and as a vehicle for spiritual practice. It was for this reason that we met in a Paris airport, just before he was due to return to the United States. First, however, I wanted to know where Ram Dass felt himself to be now, after twenty-five years and more of spiritual practice and search.

In response, he pointed out the difficulty – and the danger – of trying to assess the stages of inner experience, even though they were described in so much of the Buddhist and Hindu literature.

'It's so hard to define,' he went on. 'You know you are somewhere between awakening and enlightenment, but there is so much deceit and guile in the mind, in the way it interprets inner experience. I just know that in terms of the last twenty-five years there have been inward changes, so that the seeds of personal history and continuity have disappeared for the most part. So all I feel is the present moment, and a certain indifference, interestingly enough, to where I am. There are ways I can look at it from many planes to answer the question. First of all I am in a 58-year-old body, and that has in it certain ways of seeing the outer incarnation. I see the main body of my work as not completed, but in a later stage, and so I see now ahead of me a deeper, more reflective period, if my life goes on.'

He sat back for a moment, eyes closed. 'I see the inner

places that I am not,' he said. 'I see the equanimity isn't deep enough, nor the emptiness. Kalu Rimpoche told me there's three things for me to do in this lifetime: honour my guru, deepen my emptiness and deepen my compassion. The last two are where my work still lies. I think I honour my guru, at least as much as I know how, though that may get deeper also.

'The journey of compassion is the one that has fascinated me most because it feels most like my doorway through ... it's the door of Hanuman, it's my lineage. The question that always keeps me fascinated is how compassion arises out of emptiness and the feeling that as my clinging mind lightens I can begin to feel compassion arising out of a deeper place, and I can feel the aversions in me to poverty, illness, dying, violence, and so on; to duplicity, to paranoia. I can feel all those things still in me. I can feel my middle-class attachments still functioning.'

'Do you think, though,' I asked, ' – you're describing the personality – do you think that should or indeed could ever go? Is that actually the question?'

'It may not go in the sense of not being noticeable, but it won't colour one's behaviour quite as much. I feel ... the reason I am going to New York this fall to spend more time with the homeless is because I feel there are some places in me ready to fall away that will do so as I start to go into political meetings around housing and have to deal with angry activists; or as I go into shelters and deal with homeless people whose minds are floating around and who may be full of anger and self-pity. How much I can keep my heart open in these conditions is like my exam for awakening, for seeing where I am. I feel that is an edge for my work at this point.'

'What is it about the way of service in particular that moves you?' I asked.

'I'd say that particular path seems most appropriate to me as a Westerner,' replied Ram Dass, 'with the kind of mind and cultural background I have. It also transforms righteousness into something higher. It takes a sense of social and political responsibility into something higher. I feel like my guru charged me in that direction, by telling me to serve and feed people, so...'

'What do you feel to be the main obstacles to compassion in yourself?' I asked. 'Where do you find yourself getting caught?'

'I almost feel that the worst obstacle is my impatience, and my wishing it were done sooner, and being unwilling to be at peace with what I have got – this constant evaluating, that I am not good enough for the task in hand. I think . . . I could say my meditations weren't deep enough, but I can feel that that is a place where I am doing it to myself again. It's the judging mind that is an obstacle, in the sense that I am imagining I should be doing something I'm not doing, or that it should be different than it is. It's not a very productive stance.'

'Nevertheless it continues . . .' I suggested.

'Nevertheless it continues, because it is fed by my psychodynamics, and the culture's psychodynamics – the dis-ease in the culture . . . of somehow, what we are doing or where we are is wrong, it should be different. At moments, I know that there is nothing wrong, and it shouldn't be different, and it is all doing fine, including my doing what I am doing. When that happens I am in rhythm with the evolving process and I am . . . I really feel that the principal task is listening to the deeper harmonies, hearing one's unique form in the mosaic of human endeavour, rather than in jumping ahead out of compulsion or judgement. Listening is the optimum stance.'

'Do you feel rested in the feeling that you have found your unique form?'

'Well,' answered Ram Dass, 'I am feeling I am in line with what is. When I run my life through Maharaji's consciousness, or through hearing my options, skills, and all that, it feels okay. I don't feel I am out of balance, or I ought to be somewhere else, or doing something else. It's still very liquid, in the sense that I don't have a model of where I am going or what I should be doing or how it is all going to turn out. I mean I don't know whether Seva is going to be a cul-de-sac. At the moment I can feel the growth, but it may stop at any second. I don't know whether my work with Aids is short-term, or going to go deeper. I don't know whether my spiritual teaching is coming to an end and I'll be primarily political – social, or whether that stage in its turn will simply run its course in a year or two and then I'm going to realise that my particular dharma has to do with the deeper sufferings that have to do with the clingings of mind rather than the sufferings that have to do with hunger and shelter. It's hearing what you uniquely can do . . .

'Now I am doing more the things that other people can do, and that is more like riding the big wave; but if you want to ride the little wave in front . . . if you have less fear than others, you can ride further out in front of the wagon train. As I ride closer to the mainstream, society says, "Ram Dass, you're wonderful, you are contributing, you are great" – that's fine, but at the same time lots of people can do that. I just feel I am a little lazy in a way when I settle in at that speed.'

I could imagine his feeling like this. Here was a man, after all, who had spent a significant part of his life in the cultural vanguard. I remarked that it was now more a question of what was revolutionary becoming a mainstream way of seeing.

'Yes,' he replied, 'but the revolutionary part is to do with breaking with (self-) righteousness. Now that's scary, because that is when you lose the support of society. Society no longer sees you as a good guy then; they just don't understand you. Then you are a teacher for the few instead of the many, and the whole game is different; you are getting into the area of amorality, which is very frightening for most people, and that is a leading edge.'

I wanted to return to the question of service. I remarked that whatever form it took it seemed to be a particularly appropriate spiritual practice in the West today because it was a secular activity. We no longer had, after all, a religious tradition that held the imagination of the culture.

This was clearly an issue to which Ram Dass had given considerable thought. He began to speak animatedly. 'You are now raising the other issue,' he said, 'which is, "What is the relation between service and spiritual practice?" And whether or not a Gandhi or a Mother Teresa actually brings people closer to God or whether they are simply perceived as people doing good works, like the Quakers. Whether or not it brings people into the spirit, where the surcease of suffering really is, is something else. I am really interested in enunciating a karma yoga for this time and *zeitgeist*, that not only relieves suffering of a physical and psychological kind, but attends to the root cause of suffering, both for the servers and those who are served. I don't know that this is enunciated yet in our culture. I don't even know that it can be done. What metaphysical basis is necessary? The ideas of reincarnation and evolution – are these necessary for effective karma yoga, or can they be dispensed with? Is it necessary to see the one you are serving as the Beloved, or is it simply an added condition? I haven't worked out what the essential conditions are for karma yoga to work, in terms of it being work on oneself.'

I made the comment that service was normally interpreted in a rather narrow sense – such as feeding the hungry, or caring for the sick – in which case it excluded the many people who were not temperamentally suited to doing that kind of work.

'However,' said Ram Dass immediately, 'service is really heart-to-heart resuscitation, and that can be done anywhere, in the office, with your kids, your partner, opponent, competitor, customer, supermarket attendant – that's done by the nature of your being from moment to moment . . .'

'So . . . sparking your own heart and therefore the hearts of others,' I said.

'Exactly,' Ram Dass replied. 'Once you are resting in your heart – not the emotional heart but the deeper heart, then your being resonates with other hearts, so then you are continually an environment for the healing of other beings, just by walking down the street. When we quiet down to hear that intuitive heart, when we trust it and have faith in our connection to the higher wisdom because of being part of the unity of all things . . . when there is faith about unity in the same way we have faith about diversity and our separateness

– that faith is based on our sense data – when the intuitive faith is equal or even stronger, then we start to trust our own wisdom. Then all of our acts are dharmic acts, that is they keep bringing things to unity because they are coming out of the truth of unity.'

I mentioned that what we were talking about brought to mind the Beyond Success Programme that Ram Dass had been running for the business community.

'Yes,' he said, 'that programme explored the merchant mentality and the marketing of spirituality. I said that TM, for example, gave people a mantra which promised them deeper equanimity, so more effectiveness in business; but in the process of doing the mantra, the meaning of the goals changed, so that it was a come-on to the values people had, and converting them. If we look at what those values are that people generally hold, it's not just money – it's happiness, feeling at home in the world, feeling peaceful, joyful . . . So you can say, "Look, you can see in your own life and those around you that getting more of everything doesn't actually pay off in terms of the bottom line – of what you really want. It's alienating you from others, it makes you see your employers or your employees as "them", your competitors as "them", your business partners as "them". Then you get so busy your family starts complaining and you see them as "them", and your children as "them" because you are a different generation. Pretty soon you are totally alienated and successful. So you have won and you have lost. Your strategy in this case just isn't an intelligent one. Most people get addicted to their means of getting to the goals and lose sight of the goal.'

'Wouldn't it be something,' I said, 'to have an organisation that actually lived out that heart to heart connection as its primary goal?'

'That is what Seva has attempted to do,' Ram Dass replied. 'An organisation, which is the creation of mind, has a very short half-life of spirit usually, unless you keep reinvesting it. The way Seva has been set up is to focus on relieving suffering and at the same time to perceive the deeper causes of suffering. It's really an experiment as a Karma Yoga

Institute. We have to grow through doing the service as well as help those we are serving to grow through being served. In this case the means and the end are the same, so the actual practice of running the foundation and doing the work is itself the end. It has got to be satisfying, fulfilling, and not something we burn out on by getting over-busy and over-righteous trying to do good. It's a hard one, because the more good you do the more people want you to do, and the more you have to deal with your guilt for not doing good enough . . . it's a continuous dance you're in.'

Ram Dass went on to say that in the 1960s everyone had been keen to set up alternative institutions, and that in some ways, Seva was a throwback to that time. Many people had learned in the mean time that if they continued to work in existing social structures, there was nevertheless the possibility of change from within that structure – change not only for the individual but for the social structure as well. A friend of his was working in the Pentagon in Washington, and had a meditation group numbering almost 200 within the Pentagon itself. When the Russian generals had come over, a part of the Russian contingent had met with the meditation group and they had meditated together. Ram Dass's friend had just done this persistently over five or ten years and it had gone on gathering strength. 'I can feel that people who have evolved in their own being,' Ram Dass continued, 'can go into social situations where the whole game seems hostile to the deeper truths, and just in the quality of their being, without ever talking metaphysics, they can act in a way which brings people closer to the spirit. They can do it in hospitals, in businesses, anywhere. One of the main themes of my life is Gandhi's dictum, "My life is my message", the idea that the way you walk down the street or eat your lunch is part of what it is that transforms human beings around you. Now that is the advanced stage of karma yoga. In the early stages you do need to put a fence around the tree because it's very little. Later on it can give shade to everyone and a fence isn't needed.'

'What kind of fence are you thinking of?' I asked.

'In the early stages you need satsang,' Ram Dass replied.

'You need to be around other people who are sharing your values. At that stage you can't really expect to be able to spend all your time working for the telephone company and not go under. But as time goes on you may begin to handle the telephone company, or even the political arena – you could be in politics. Recently I was with Jerry Brown, who used to be Governor of California, and who was running for President a few years back. Now he has just been sitting Zen in Japan and working with Mother Teresa in Calcutta and he wants to be back in politics now. I said that the only interesting way to be in politics, to my mind, is to be free enough of your own desire for worldly power that you can bring to politics a quality of compassion that is not vulnerable to the situation. In that context the tiniest conceit in you gets magnified immensely. I suggested he go back to his meditation cushion and also do service for another five years, and see how he was then. After all, if your power needs are played out, what's the rush?'

'If one were wanting to see one's work, whatever it may be, as a means of practice, where would one start?' I asked.

'I think you'd start by setting aside fifteen to twenty minutes a day to reflect about your day in the light of your deeper wishes and intentions. If you take a passage from some sacred text, for example, and reflect on your day in the light of this; if you just did that every day and nothing else, change would begin to occur. Love thy neighbour as thyself – take that one, and look at what you did the day before, where you lost it, where you remembered. It's vital of course not to get judgemental. Just see what is there. Just keep juxtaposing some metaphysical truth alongside what you do every day. There is another way,' he added, 'take the actual condition you are in, and use techniques to re-perceive them while you are in them. That is not in retrospect, but in the actual moment. Mantra can be about this, or the practice of seeing the Beloved in everyone you work with; also seeing the way your own mind grabs and pushes away at any given moment.'

'One of the struggles in our culture today is to make a

living that provides meaning,' I said. 'Would you comment on that?'

Ram Dass closed his eyes again for a moment, as if he were taking the question inside. 'I think that you listen for the meaning of the moment,' he said finally, 'You listen ... and you hear what your opportunities are, what situation you find yourself in, what your skills are, what the truth of your being at that moment is. The closer you stay to that truth the quicker it all transforms. The more you get phony-holy, the more you cut yourself off. The more you stay overlong in your mind, and are preoccupied with what you think you ought to be doing rather than what you are doing, the more you move away from yourself. When you listen in and you find you are a bus driver, if you are quiet enough to feel the suffering of the people getting on the bus, you feel your empathy, your own poor salary, your own frustrations and you sit with what you've got, and it is as if there is a meaning inherent in the way the whole picture is evolving. It's as if the formless coming into form brings with it its own doorway back into the formless. In the case of someone who has no metaphysical foundation at all, however, who is totally materialist, it is difficult for me to imagine where they derive meaning from. So that makes me a less effective spokesperson for that kind of person.'

'And yet a lot of social action is actually carried out by people like that,' I commented.

'Exactly,' Ram Dass replied. 'And that is why I feel I need to hang out with these people, and feel the truth of their being, and find out how they are me and I am them and how we can talk and be together. In *How Can I Help?* we tried to look at the question of who it is who thinks they are doing service. The whole idea of seeing it as a play, of fulfilling roles without identifying with them, these are things that can be heard psychodynamically. They don't have to be heard spiritually. A lot of organisations, like Est, for example, in my mind simply imitate spiritual truths at a psychodynamic level. That makes everyone feel they have got somewhere, which in itself is an egoic, self-satisfaction, little more. I am horrified at the prospect that I, too, perhaps, solidify the ego against the spirit by pre-empting spiritual language as an ego language.'

I made the observation that all language was in some degree the work of the conceptual mind. What distinguished a live message from a dead one was whether or not the vehicle of language was a carrier of something other than the vehicle itself . . . a carrier of spirit.

'Exactly,' Ram Dass agreed. 'In a good lecture or discussion, even though the vehicle is the words and the metaphors, the real thing that is happening is the being that is being conveyed. Through the nature of the being, there comes a point when we are all here, together in the room, and the audience tastes something at that moment that is not conceptual. Now, when this happens, I have seen how most of them immediately conceptually reduce it, almost as they are walking out of the hall, because they want to get hold of what it was. That immediately reduces it to trivia, and you wonder if it did any good at all to give the lecture in the first place. Did it increase their yearning for That, or did it just trivialise it? I love the issue, and I don't understand or know the answer at all. I mean, I think I am a little too mushy-headed about what really is, so that to those who are ready it is apparent that nothing is necessary, and to those that aren't nothing is possible. I think that if you say it well enough, people are able to hear the truth, but they are not necessarily able to use it immediately. After all, I heard truths twenty-five years ago with drugs that I still can't use. So if I, who spend a good deal of my time trying to understand all this, have a hard time sometimes, what can I expect from people who have to spend all their time and energy working for a living? Mind you,' he mused, 'I haven't made the hardest effort, because of my karma, no doubt, and also because when I go to make a hard effort, the patent fallacy of trying to make it stops me. As Maharaji said, if someone wants God, then let them just tie rocks to themselves and jump in the water. If you are doing it for God you will get God. If you are doing it to avoid life, it is called suicide. Most people don't want God that badly. They just stay with the feeling of wanting to want God.'

This, I reflected, was being said by someone who had made far more effort than most. I returned to the point Ram Dass had made about the psychodynamic imitation of spiritual language. Surely, I said, that was all that could be done for the most part, since people needed to start from where they were, which was, after all, the psychological domain of the ego.

'Well, yes,' he replied, 'and right to the end that is going to be the truth of it – for as long as there is spiritual practice there will be psychodynamics. There has got to be somebody doing the practices, and that somebody is somebody-ness, the ego. Chogyam Trungpa's line on that is just brilliant, that enlightenment is the ego's ultimate disappointment.'

'Do you ever feel despair in the face of the impossibility of it all?' I asked ' – of ever actually being able to deal in any lasting sense with the suffering of the world, or with your own suffering?'

Ram Dass laughed. 'No,' he answered, 'because I really do feel it's all quite perfect, and I am not sure anything should change. I just know I have to be an instrument for change, but whether it should change is none of my business. I know if Maharaji wants it to change then it will do so, and if he doesn't, then it won't. I trust the game, basically – I think it's more interesting than anything I'm doing, so ... I just feel part of a process, and if it's not the time, then ... this just may not be the time for that kind of awakening. Last year I really felt it was a generational cycle, and that we were in the next generation after the post '60s one, and that it was all starting again – people were waking up again. But I now realise that it wasn't actually coming from a deep enough place of yearning, so I was overestimating what seemed to be going on. So I need to listen more carefully to the truth of the culture we are working with. I may be a voice, along with Seva, that is only going to be heard thirty years from now, even long after I am dead. Well, that's fine with me, I am just going to keep feeding the stuff in. When the Third Patriarch of Zen wrote his tract, he was treated like a bum, and certainly not given much respect and honour...'

'Far less than you are given at present...'

'Far less . . . yet his message kept resonating because it was connected with truth. I think that truth is what the issue is, and if you keep feeding it, then that is the best you can do, and the results will look after themselves. After all,' Ram Dass continued, 'we are in the age of the kali yuga, the age of spiritual darkness. Now if life on earth is a school, then the kali yuga is an exquisite curriculum, and just remembering the name of God in the kali yuga is already . . . I mean you're already almost home. More so than if you were doing wonderful Gregorian chants your whole life in some other age.'

'How many of us can remember the name of God for one hour . . .?' I remarked.

Ram Dass smiled. 'Or even for one minute with full faith,' he said.

'And yet, you know,' he continued, as we got up to check in for his flight, 'I do have a very deep faith that we are all involved in an evolutionary process, and that evolution is at the level of the individual entity. I feel the truth of that, and that evolution is inevitable and irrevocable. How it all unfolds I have no idea. I just try and bring whatever consciousness I can about it all, through my quietness, to facilitate the whole unfolding. But so few people get enlightened. Five billion people on the planet, and barely a handful, maybe, known what enlightenment is. What a mysterious thing, that it should be that way.'

— 18 —

Meditation

Over the centuries, the many shapes and forms of what is now known as meditation have filled a thousand books in as many languages. I am about to follow a short way in the footsteps of Lao Tsu, who, having said that he who speaks does not know, proceeded to say more than most on this and similar subjects.

One may be forgiven for wondering why a book whose subject is everyday life conceived as spiritual practice ends with a chapter and a discussion on meditation. It is not, in fact, incongruous. Interiority is the natural and necessary complement for an active life in the world. It is when we follow one direction to the exclusion of the other that the result can be one of opposition.

I see meditation to be a principal way of giving us the taste of both a clarity and a luminous presence that can remind us of what is also a possibility within the heart of daily activity. On the other hand, it gives us a sobering reflection of our normal everyday condition, which we are often too embroiled in to notice. Then, meditation happens with and in the body; it is a direct means of experiencing the fusion of the worlds of form and the formless. Finally, it has been the single most constant undertaking in my life, and I know that its action on me has been instrumental in shaping the attitudes and perspectives that fill this book.

I did not come to meditation as a Buddhist, a Christian, or anything in particular. It has been there as long as I can remember – not known to me in the beginning as 'meditation' as such – some method or other that one can practise – but as a simple facility for slipping into the spaciousness behind thoughts.

As a university student I used to find myself sitting quietly, eyes open, falling into a state of silent communion with the natural environment. One of my courses at the time was on Stendhal and I found great reward in discovering in his pages various descriptions of what he called *'moments de bonheur'* – moments that mirrored my own sense of innocence and delight in simply 'being with' what I was with.

Far from being a withdrawal from the world, the activity was one of entering more fully and deeply into it, so that I and my environment were part of the same unity. The return to ordinary, dualistic consciousness was accompanied with a sense of having been profoundly nourished, and, at times, with a certain sadness.

I can see now how this state of 'falling in' often merged into something else, something quite different – the dreamer, the one who preferred the sweet reverie of fleeting, uplifting emotional states to the opacity of matter and its attendant commitments and responsibilities. Even this dreaming figure, though, has a truth of his own: he knows that the world as experienced solely through the rational, purposeful and strategic self, is hollow and not really alive. Accompanying this is a sense of Life, meaning, fulness, existing elsewhere than in this everyday realm. With this intuition, it is not surprising that the dreamer began to form in my psyche, and to steal a portion of my life energy.

What I mean by meditation, though, is to be distinguished from the activity of the dreamer. It is first and foremost a penetration into – no, a progressively deeper recognition of – the depths of what is already actually Here. The most natural relationship with any deeper, fuller sense of life has not, in my case, been an attempt to penetrate anything, to aspire upwards, to pierce the veil; but to be open, receptive and attentive to the degree that Whatever Is might reveal itself in me, and in that sense, remind me What Is. Life is Present, immanent. It is I who am usually not Here, and the act of sitting is a means to bring me round.

There are a bewildering number of meditation techniques which aim to do this in different ways, and which are amply described in the language and orientation of every spiritual tradition. Which specific path we choose or bump into is usually a matter of individual disposition. What we shall discuss here, rather than a particular method, is primarily the underlying attitudes that we bring to meditation in the first place. The inner posture towards whatever we are doing very largely determines our experience of the activity itself. A Buddhist may say they are practising meditation to arrive at enlightenment; a Christian, that they are opening to God; a Sufi or a Hindu might want to sail out of the body altogether on the wings of absorption and return full of bliss and the ineffable. Whatever the different rationales and methods may be, there are certain attitudes towards meditation that are to be found in every single tradition. These are inherent to the nature of meditation itself, and even, perhaps, indispensable to it.

The theme that has been most consistently apparent in meditation for me is unknowing. What drew me to the actual practice of meditation, as distinct to the spontaneous facility for it, was partly a sense of my ignorance and bewilderment in the face of my daily experience of life itself. There are times when, usually through the force of outward circumstance, I catch a glimpse of my dispersion and my manifest incapability to understand the influences at work in my life; what I am doing here, who I am, or where I am going, if anywhere. From this arises the desire to know, along with the memory that I have come into a degree of knowing in the past by sitting still in one place, and, in the first instance, returning to myself.

Yet neither, in sitting down, do I know what I am sitting down to. Certainly there are steps to be gone through that quieten the body and slow the mind, and that can bring me more into the present moment. It is not just a question, though, of experiencing life in its material forms as more real, more alive. It is not a question of quantity at all. Meditation can open a door on to qualities and dimensions that are quite other than bodily life altogether, even though known in and through the body. What was at first most conscious for me as a strain of something akin to pantheism, a communion with and through natural forms and the environment, began with more consistent sitting to accrue a sense of Otherness, and of Vastness. At times there was the sensation of being before an Unknown which acted upon me like a magnet, drawing me to it in the degree that I was able – or dared – to turn in its direction. At other times, there has been only the intention (to or for what I cannot quite say), entering or falling into a darkness, or a transparent nothing, like a tiny dart into a vast night sky. In either case – and the distinction is by no means as clear as I appear to have made it here – the darkness has thickened the more I have faced it. Facing it is not always easy. Usually there is an apprehension, a trembling of the mind, if not the body, at the intimation of its possible undoing. What we are turning to, after all, is in one way familiar somehow; and yet at the same time utterly Unknown; Present, yet stretching far beyond anything I know as presence.

There is a more frequent unknowing which knows nothing of presence or a trembling mind. Often the task is to be willing to sit in the midst of the awareness of our lack – our lack of any real motivation, of any particular feeling other than, perhaps, boredom or frustration. Just sitting with this, not trying to change it or do anything about it, and not judging it either; just watching it can open a broader view. The broader view, though, still has nothing on the horizon, not even darkness, and certainly no consolations. This simple, arduous sitting is for no reason; there is nowhere to go, and the sense of absence is sufficient in itself, although even this is not clung to. For Thomas Merton, this was the prayer of the desert, the deepest prayer of all.

> Contemplative prayer is, in a way, simply the preference for the desert, for emptiness, for poverty ... Only when we are able to 'let go' of everything within us, all desire to see, to know, to taste and to experience the presence of God, do we truly become able to experience that presence with the overwhelming conviction and reality that revolutionize our entire inner life.[31]

Another theme common to all forms of meditation is the paradox of needing to make an effort on the one hand, and to be receptive and available on the other. There is an old Sufi saying which points to the razor's edge that we need to follow:

If you seek Him you shall never find Him.
If you do not seek Him,
He will never reveal Himself to you.

Something needs to be done; some gesture needs to be made; yet if I push too hard or in the wrong way I will create more resistance than I started with. Our intention is normally tied to a method, be it following the breath, repeating a name, or resting one's eyes on a white wall. While keeping our attention on the method, without straining or forcing ourselves, we are also called to remain in a posture of openness and availability to ourselves, and to whatever it is that arises; to the thoughts and the feelings that we would rather not hear, or to the recurring ache in the knee.

There is a deeper availability still; to that which stands behind and beyond any method we may be using. Here we come upon the themes of offering and surrender. All that we have may be our discomfort and pain; or our dispersion and scattered will; or we may have the fire of a burning intention, or the quiet wish to enter the silence. Whatever our experience, meditation calls us to offer it up; to surrender it to – to What? To whatever it is that lies beyond our experience, and is therefore, for the present, greater or other than we can know. Ultimately, even the sense of the Void, of Presence, of the nearness of the One, of unfathomable silence; even the deepest state we can know needs to be offered into the Question itself. Meditation will always point further than where we are.

Everything we are speaking of will always have its reflection in the body. The body is the anchor and ground for any meditation we may practise. It is the body, first of all, that can enable us to return to ourselves, to the moment we are in. As we become aware of the sensations in our legs, our abdomen and chest, the whole body, we can release the tremors of any unfinished responses to a previous situation; we can begin to be where we are, just sitting.

If one can simply park one's body in one spot for half an hour or more without altering the posture, something can begin to happen. The body can begin to hold the mind, which in its turn can then settle down. This is not to say that the body is forced into a rigid position, but that it is allowed to speak for itself. Given the opportunity, it can begin to express its own natural receptivity to the deeper influences of meditation. As we allow the posture to be softly erect, open across the shoulders, with a free neck, and anchored in the legs with the breathing in the belly; so we begin to be more attentive and available, which in its turn allows the body to release its tensions and be drawn upwards and outwards while still being rooted to the ground.

If we give attention to the sensation in our body from head to toe, aware of it as a complete form, it can become progressively stiller, 'held' somehow, assuming the form of a vessel. As the silence descends the attention heightens, or perhaps the other way around. At this point, the attention may remain gathered at the level of a relative silence of body and mind, with a slow procession of thoughts intermittently coming and going. Or the silence can go deeper so that any awareness of thought ceases and there is only a solid, stable, dark silence in which both body and mind are held, as if suspended. There is still awareness of the body, but as a statue, firm, erect, with energy sometimes moving up and down and around it, but immobile. In these moments, the body itself may feel like a wordless offering into the silence. At times, it can feel as if the body, one's very being, is being imprinted in some way; as if one were, for want of better words, being modelled, 'made good', and drawn into a state of contemplation through the entire body.

These states are among the innumerable ones that may arise as we move more deeply into practice. They are not, as we have already said, the goal. The purpose is rather to travel on, without lingering too long at the wayside inns – though the inns have their purpose, too, as providers of sustenance along the way.

Though this chapter has been titled 'Meditation', I have used the word only because of its current coinage. Meditation refers more properly to a technique of some kind that can act as a staff of support. There are other words, which though encumbered with the baggage of outworn tradition, are nevertheless more appropriate and accurate for the deeper stages of what we have been describing: contemplation, for example, and even prayer, in a certain way. Here, though, what we are pointing to is a wordless prayer of the whole body; not a plea to some vague entity, but a silent gesture of receptivity to the mystery and immensity of Life itself.

Irina Tweedie

Irina Tweedie

Irina Tweedie, at 82, is one of the most passionate people I have ever met. Anyone who has read her book *Chasm of Fire*, will understand why. All her secondary loves have been worn away by her love for the One Beloved. This final chapter is dedicated to her because I realise that if I can put any name at all to the journey I have been tracing, it is the journey of the lover. By the lover, I mean a response to life that would dare to open its arms and say yes to the unknown, whatever form it may take. Love itself comes from the unknowable, from far beneath and beyond our conscious mind; and it aspires madly to rejoin the mystery of its source.

Irina Tweedie has been drawn like a moth to the call of that mystery for more than twenty years; ever since she lived in India beside a Sufi saint who extinguished in her all desire for anything other than the love for God. When I first met her, ten years ago, her house was filled every week with fifty students, who came to meditate with her. Now her house is crammed with a hundred people every week, and she has large groups of students in Germany and America. She herself, however, rarely leaves her house, and certainly makes no attempt to increase her popularity. People are simply attracted by the magnetic force of her love for life's source.

I met her again recently after an interval of several years. She seemed hardly changed; still the same concern for my welfare, the immediate tea and biscuits; the joy at the sight of a bird in the garden; and at the same time, an inner authority which brought with it the inescapable feeling that the tea, the bird, our meeting, me, her own words, left no permanent trace on her inner landscape. How difficult it is to describe the presence of fullness and emptiness at one and the same time. I wanted to talk to her about meditation.

Mrs Tweedie, as she is known, is Russian. Still, after the larger part of a lifetime in Britain, she has the rich and melodious Russian accent.

'Meditation,' she replied, 'is the experience of absolute stillness, darkness, and nothingness. It is ultimately oneness with something that is nothing. In a way, sufi meditation is not really meditation at all. If we meditate we meditate upon something. In our case, however, we leave the mind completely behind us in order to enter the uncreated, dark light of God. We pass into a state where the mind is thrown into the universal mind. This feels like unconsciousness at the beginning. We gradually wake up out of this into a degree of superconsciousness, though this normally takes many years.'

I wanted to clarify her last statement. 'We are waking up, then,' I suggested, 'from our smaller identity into our larger one?'

'Exactly. Our mind is made in such a way that we receive our impressions from outside. As soon as you think, there is the thought and there is you. In deep meditation, there is not you and the knowledge: you are the knowledge, so there is no duality. There are different states. There are moments of oneness with the Beloved, absolute ecstasy and bliss. That is nothingness. And this nothingness loves you, responds to you, fulfills you utterly and yet there is nothing there. You flow out like a river, without diminishing. This is the great mystical experience, the great ecstasy. Neither does it happen at your will, it is a grace. You may decide to go into meditation, but those moments of Oneness when It wants you, that is different: then you are seized. It is a very erotic experience, not felt in the sexual organs but in the throat chakra. It is felt as a constant streaming out in glorious bliss, and something coming in to you in response. This is the best I can say, but it is misleading. This is why the Sufis use erotic imagery in their poetry.

'Our relationship with God,' she continued, 'is that of the

lover with the Beloved, the flight of one to the One. It is an
infinitely intimate relationship. You would not speak of
others when you are in bed with the most beloved woman.
So the Sufis do not speak of it directly. It would be a
blasphemy. It is an erotic experience; not a sexual one, but an
ecstatic one, mainly in the throat, but all over the body.
Every cell, full of light, becomes happy in its own right. I
cannot say more than that.'

Nor could I. Mrs Tweedie had brought the quality of what
she was speaking about into the room. I turned the conversation in a slightly different direction.

'The whole Judao-Christian, as well as the Islamic, tradition,' I said, 'is steeped in this language of lover and
relationship. Buddhist Vipassana meditation, however, takes
a very different route, in which there is no relationship with
anything beyond one's own breath or thought stream. The
purpose of Vipassana is to reveal our inherent lack of
identity, and insubstantiality. These are radically different
approaches, aren't they?'

'Yes, but when you are united with the Beloved in the
night, when you seem to die, there is nothing there, nothing
at all. There is no contradiction in the end. It is the most
intimate relationship, yet the mind knows nothing of it. You
may have this experience that you cannot articulate. So you
try to set the same thing up again. You sit in the same way,
you adjust the environment as before, and what happens?
Your experience this time is entirely different. There is
nothing you can grasp hold of. When I first awoke into what
I can only call a superconscious state in meditation, I was
expecting to find God, because I was conditioned by my
Christian upbringing. But there was no God. There was
nothing. An infinity of light. That's all. But it changed me
forever. For years my mind could not grasp what had
happened.'

'You crossed over the threshold of fear, then, which allows
you to accept that there is – that you are – no-thing.'

'People are afraid of nothingness,' Mrs Tweedie replied,
'but it is nothingness only for the mind. The Isha Upanishad
speaks of the eternal fullness, which is the Pleroma of the

ancient Greeks. If you take fullness away from fullness, fullness alone remains. This nothingness is the deepest fulfilment. It sounds like double-Dutch, but when you realise it, it is utterly obvious and natural. You are loved like no one in the world can love you and yet you are already dead. There is a beautiful simile in the Bhagavata Purana when Krishna was dancing with 16,000 gopis, the milkmaids, and every one of them thought she had him all to herself. The real experiencer is the Atman. In sexual intercourse it is really the soul, not the body that is the experiencer. The moment of ultimate ecstasy in sex is beyond this world. That is why it is so powerful, and human beings run after it, even commit crime for it, because of this moment, so elusive and so brief. In deep samadhi, however, it can last all night. In samadhi, as in sexuality, the body is very much involved. You have to surrender, but also physically. Every cell sheds its light in samadhi.'

'How might a human relationship,' I asked, 'mirror this greater relationship in samadhi.'

'In sexual intercourse, if you really deeply love. But you must love deeply. It could not happen in a one-night adventure. Isn't world literature full of comparisons between human love and the love of God? It is a lifelong work, though, and a rare thing. The couple must woo and conquer each other in every moment. A marriage is a constant effort.'

'You have quoted Hindu literature, but some of the expressions you use also sound quite Christian. You could almost be describing contemplative Christian practices.'

'Of course. I remember when I first came back from India in 1963 I read St Teresa. The human soul has no frontiers you see. St Gregory of Nyssa said as much. "The path of love is like a bridge of hair across a chasm of fire." He also said, "You go up the hill and you see still higher ones. Then you have to go down to go still higher." There is no end to it. Spiritual life is so unbelievable. It keeps you so young. I am in love like a sixteen-year-old girl,' she laughed. 'Yet in love with what?'

I asked her if the bliss she was speaking of could also be an obstacle to something which transcended even bliss. Bliss was a state, after all, and all states are transient.

Mrs Tweedie nodded. She said that her teacher had told her, when he was sending her to England, that the time would come when only love would remain and the time would also come when even love would go. Then nothing would remain. Bliss, she felt, could be an obstacle when one experienced the lower stages of it, and continually hankered after it. Ultimately, though, one couldn't help being drawn to it, because the soul was bliss and God was also bliss, or love.

I returned to the subject of meditation. 'For me,' I said, 'meditation is an act of offering into the Presence, a listening for, or into that silence. Sometimes it happens that there is no more awareness of me listening; there is just empty space and the awareness of it. I haven't gone unconscious or gone out of the body, but there is a stillness which descends which is tangible, which is more alive than anything I ordinarily know.'

Mrs Tweedie was gazing at me intently. 'This is exactly the right attitude to my mind,' she said. 'It is the attitude of surrender, and surrender is sine qua non the most important ingredient of the spiritual path. This is the goal of yogic contentment. You are surrendered. You have nothing more to do. It takes over. You have emptied your cup and something else has been able to come in.'

'Surrendered to what, though?' I asked.

'It is impossible to name. It is just *It*. That It is something, and it loves you, and you are never alone any more, never. Mind you, sometimes He hides Himself behind a veil. You just can't meditate sometimes, and you are sitting in front of a brick wall. We call it the yo yo syndrome – one day everything is wonderful, and the next . . . nothing.'

I wanted to pursue my previous question. 'When I say meditation is an offering,' I said, 'what is it that is being offered?'

'What you are really offering,' Mrs Tweedie replied, 'is your own ego, the little self. That is the crucifixion. That's why what I described in my book was so difficult for me. I struggled and struggled. Now I know better. Now I am able to say thy will be done. That's all. You come to the point where the Beloved is everything and the lover is dead.

Nothing else matters. What happens then is another matter. There comes a time when you no longer have the desire to tell others who they are. Simply dare to say thy will be done. That's the hardest step for the ego because the ego has to go. It doesn't go, anyway, it changes. Carl Jung said you can't become anything else than what you are. The whole thing is a process of alchemical transformation. Only surrender does it. And it is painful because the ego will fight back. If you don't fight back and just say here I am, you will sense a great smile, and your heart will smile in return.'

'The ego of course is invaluable for daily existence, as is the process of thought,' I added. 'I imagine that what you are pointing to embraces the ego and our everyday life, rather than removing us from it?'

'Certainly,' Mrs Tweedie said. 'Sufis are not allowed to go in solitude. They have to realise the truth within the conditions of ordinary existence that our higher self has put us in. The world and all its temptations will close tightly around us, and within it we must realise the truth. The greater the limitation, the greater the perfection. In other words, the devil is very useful if you can overcome him.'

'So everyday life is the ashram?'

'Absolutely. There is really no such thing as the material world and the spiritual world. At the beginning they will seem to be different, but later there is no difference. The one is a mirror image of the other.'

'How, then,' I asked, 'can the meditation we have spoken of affect everyday life?'

'To begin with,' Mrs Tweedie replied, 'one's values change. What was important now no longer seems so. The teacher and the practice represent completely different values and these begin to influence you.'

'What kind of values are you speaking of?'

'Greed, for example, intellectual greed as well as material greed, loses its value. I suffered greatly from intellectual greed. I passed exam after exam, just for the sake of knowledge. I was brought up in academic circles, so it was a family habit. It's useless. The nearer you come to That which encompasses everything, the more you realise that That is all you want to know. So you love your neighbour as yourself because they *are* you. And to love yourself, what does it mean? It means to forgive yourself. Especially we women, you know. We constantly have this feeling of inadequacy, or guilt about something.'

'Even so,' I said, finally, 'it could sound from everything you have said about meditation that one comes to have no great enthusiasm for being in the world.'

'Oh no. I understand that it might seem that way but in practice, it is just the opposite. Life is never so real or beautiful. The difference is, however, that we are no longer chasing after it and its pleasures. We have the taste of something infinitely more precious. My life is at its end, but I tell you that flowers have never looked so red; nor has food ever tasted so good as it does now. And yet, I am not chasing these things, the things of the world. There is something I cannot name which is lovelier still. It is nowhere else; it is here, but it is not of this world.'

Notes

PART I

Chapter 2

1. Plato, *The Symposium*, 281 A-B, quoted in Borna Bebek, *The Third City*, Methuen Books, London, 1982, p. 120.
2. Ibid.
3. Quoted by P. L. Travers, 'Green Grow the Rushes', *Parabola*, Winter 1989, p. 6.
4. Ibid.

Chapter 3

5. J. G. Bennett, *The Way To Be Free*, Coombe Springs Press, 1975.
6. Idries Shah, *Thinkers of the East*, Octagon Press, London, 1977.
7. Wendell Berry, *Standing by Words*, North Point Press, Berkeley, Ca., 1983, p. 43.
8. See Ken Wilbur's book, *Transformations of Consciousness*, Shambhala, 1986.

Chapter 5

9. Cyprian Smith, *The Way of Love and Paradox*, Darton Longman and Todd, 1987.

PART II

Chapter 7

10. A saying of Krishna quoted by Shivapuri Baba in J. G. Bennett, *Long Pilgrimage*, Turnstone Books, 1975, p. 176.

Chapter 8

11. Quoted by Cyprian Smith, *The Way of Love and Paradox*, Darton Longman and Todd, 1987, p. 24.

12. Jacob Needleman, *Lost Christianity*, Element Books, Shaftesbury, 1990, p. 37.

Chapter 9

13. From 'Preserving Wildness', in Wendell Berry, *The Landscape of Harmony*, Five Seasons Press, Hereford, 1987.
14. This paragraph owes much to Robert Bly's 'Meditation on a Poem by Yeats', in his *News of the Universe*, Sierra Club Books, San Francisco, 1980.

Chapter 11

15. Robert Bly, 'Listening to the Köln Concert', in *Loving a Woman in Two Worlds*, Harper & Row, New York, 1985.
16. Ibid., p. 68.

Chapter 13

17. Cecil Collins, 'To the Gates of the Sun', *Resurgence*, May–June 1987.
18. Suzi Gablik, *Has Modernism Failed?*, Thames & Hudson, London, 1985.

Chapter 14

19. Kathleen Raine, *Collected Poems 1935–1980*, Allen & Unwin, London, 1981, p. 261.

Chapter 15

20. Dominique Lapierre, *The City of Joy*, Arrow Books, London, 1986, p. 144.
21. Ram Dass and Paul Gorman, *How Can I Help?*, Rider, London, 1985, pp. 52–3.
22. Quoted by Peter Lamborn Wilson in 'The Bleak Garden', *Parabola*, Vol. XI, no. 3. p. 60.

Chapter 16

23. Kahhil Gibran, *The Prophet*, Alfred A. Knopf, New York, 1972, pp. 29–30.
24. Huston Smith, *Forgotten Truth*, Harper & Row, New York, 1976, p. 121.
25. Ibid., p. 130.
26. Wendell Berry, *The Landscape of Harmony*, Five Seasons Press, Hereford, 1987.

27. Richard Kearney, *The Wake of Imagination*, Century Hutchinson, 1988, p. 29.
28. J. G. Bennett, *The Way to Be Free*, Coombe Springs Press.
29. From Michael Phillips, *The Seven Laws of Money*, quoted in Nancy Anderson, *Work with Passion*, Carroll & Graf, New York, 1984, pp. 222–3.
30. Ram Dass and Paul Gorman, *How Can I Help?*, Rider, London, 1985, p. 16.

Chapter 18
31. Thomas Merton, *Contemplative Prayer*, reprinted by Darton Longman and Todd, 1975, p. 111.